KU-168-431

A B C D E F G H I J K L M

### THE ILLUSTRATED

# ENCYCLOPEDIA

## VOLUME 7



# R-S

Belitha Press

N O P Q R S T U V W X Y Z

First published 1995 by
Macmillan Education Australia Pty Ltd

First published in the United Kingdom in 1995 by
Belitha Press Limited
31 Newington Green, London N16 9PU



Cataloguing in print data available from the British Library.

ISBN 1 85561 526 6 (Vol 7)
ISBN 1 85561 529 0 (Set)

Consultant: Frances Warhurst
UK editor: Maria O'Neill
Project editor: Jo Higgins

Typeset by Polar Design
Printed in Hong Kong

## Acknowledgements

The author and publishers are grateful to the following for permission to reproduce copyright photographs:

Cover: Sporting Pix

Kevin Aitken/A.N.T. Photo Library, p. 44; Bill Bachman/A.N.T. Photo Library, p. 18 (top right); Coo-ee Picture Library, pp. 8, 9 (bottom), 11 (bottom), 13 (bottom left), 15 (left), 18 (left), 19 (left), 21 (centre left), 23 (bottom right & top left), 24 (top), 29 (top & bottom), 32 & 33, 34, 36, 39 (centre right), 46, 48 (top), 53 (top left), 55 (bottom left), 56, 61 (top right), 64 (bottom right); John Higgins, pp. 13 (top), 29 (centre); HYUNDAI, p. 27 (top); International Photographic Library, p. 13 (bottom right); Peter Krauss/A.N.T. Photo Library, p. 55 (top left); Rudie Kuiter/A.N.T. Photo Library, p. 37; NASA, pp. 35 (top), 58, 59, 62, 64 (top); Gerard Lacz/A.N.T. Photo Library, p. 30; Naval Photographic Centre, p. 63; Northside Photographs, pp. 4 & 5 (bottom), 5 (top), 7 (top), 17 (top left), 23 (bottom left), 31 (bottom right), 38, 48 (bottom left & right), 51, 53 (top right & bottom), 54, 55 (bottom right), 57; Northern Territory Tourism Commission, pp. 21 (top), 28 (bottom); N.H.P.A./A.N.T. Photo Library, pp. 5 (centre), 16 (bottom), 17 (top right & bottom), 41; Outback Photographs, p. 9 (centre); The Photo Library, p. 27 (bottom left & right); PIA/Plastic Industry Association, p. 18 (bottom centre); C & S Pollitt/A.N.T. Photo Library, p. 31 (bottom left); Otto Rogge/A.N.T. Photo Library, p. 61 (top); Silvestris/A.N.T. Photo Library, 30, 39 (top & bottom right); M.F. Sopher/A.N.T. Photo Library, p. 20 (bottom); Sporting Pix Australia, p. 24 (bottom right), 33 (top & right), 50 (bottom); Ron & Valerie Taylor/A.N.T. Photo Library, pp. 44, 53 (centre); Norbert Wu/A.N.T. Photo Library, p. 61 (bottom right).

While every care has been taken to trace and acknowledge copyright the publishers tender their apologies for any accidental infringement where copyright has proved untraceable.

**Illustrators**
Sharyn Madder: 4, 5, 14, 15, 22, 23, 24, 25, 29, 40, 41
Rhyll Plant: 10, 12, 13, 20, 21, 42, 43, 52, 53, 54, 55, 60, 61, 62, 64
John Fairbridge: 8, 9, 26, 44, 45, 46, 47, 48, 59, 63
Paul Konye: 6, 7, 19, 32, 33, 34, 35, 50, 56, 57
Andrew Plant: 16, 17, 30, 31, 37, 38, 39
Xiangyi Mo: 49, 51

# HOW TO USE THIS BOOK

*The Illustrated Encyclopedia* has over 300 entries. The entries are arranged alphabetically. To find your topic, use the guide letters at the top of each page to check you have the right volume. The first letter of your topic will be highlighted.

## TOPIC: RAIN FOREST

guide letter

N O P Q R S T U V W X Y Z

Use the guide words printed in the top right-hand corner of each page to find your topic. The guide words list the entries on a double-page spread. They are listed alphabetically. Check the guide words to see if you need to go backwards or forwards.

guide word

RAIN FOREST

You can also use the index in Volume 9 to find your topic.

rain forest
Volume 3 48–49
Volume 7 **14–15**

If you cannot find your topic in its alphabetical order in the encyclopedia, use the index.

rock pool
*see* seashore life

## TOPIC: ROCK POOL

The index lists all the topics in alphabetical order. It tells you where you will find your topic.

More information on how to use the encyclopedia and the index can be found in Volume 9.

# RABBIT

SEE ALSO • Animal • Mammal • Pet

A rabbit is a small, furry mammal that can hop. Most rabbits live in the wild. People can keep rabbits as pets.

## PARTS OF A WILD RABBIT

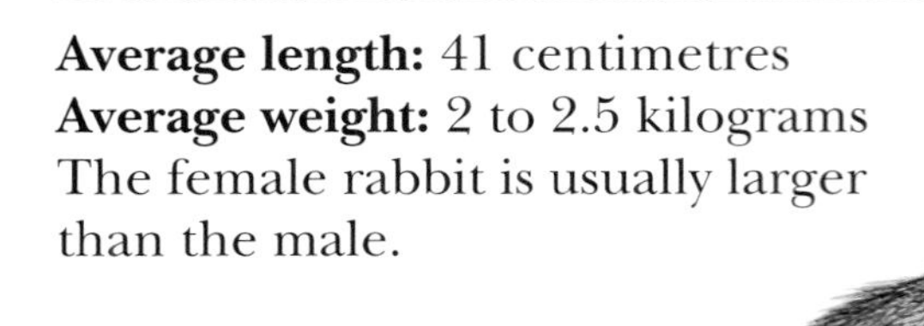

**Average length:** 41 centimetres
**Average weight:** 2 to 2.5 kilograms
The female rabbit is usually larger than the male.

long ears that can swivel to hear sounds

thick, greyish brown fur

eyes on side of the head

nose for smelling danger

white, fluffy tail to warn other rabbits of danger

sensitive whiskers to help find the way in the dark

strong long back legs for hopping

short front legs for balancing

## FOOD

Rabbits eat plants. They are herbivores.

grass

leaves

twigs

bark

roots

## WHERE RABBITS LIVE

Rabbits live in all continents except the Antarctic.

**INTERESTING FACT**

A rabbit can hop at about 30 kilometres per hour when chased by an enemy.

## **HOW** RABBITS LIVE

- Most rabbits live in large groups. They live in underground burrows called warrens.
- Most rabbits spend the day sleeping and resting. At night they come out to eat and play.
- A female rabbit usually gives birth to four to five rabbits at a time. Rabbits have several litters a year.

## RABBITS AS PESTS

Rabbits can damage farm crops and pastures. Rabbits which have been introduced to an area can destroy the places where native animals live. In the 1950s, a disease called myxomatosis which kills rabbits was used in some countries to cut down the number of rabbits.

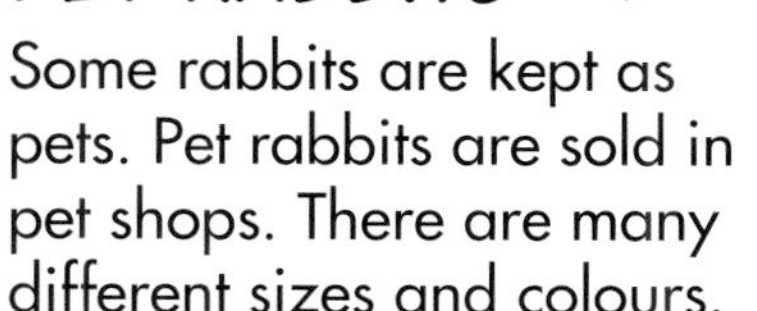

## PET RABBITS ▼

Some rabbits are kept as pets. Pet rabbits are sold in pet shops. There are many different sizes and colours.

## **DIFFERENCES** BETWEEN HARES AND RABBITS

Rabbits and hares belong to the same animal family.

- Hares are usually larger with longer back legs and larger ears.
- Newborn hares are born with fur and with their eyes open. Newborn rabbits are born bald and with their eyes closed.
- A young hare is called a leveret. A young rabbit is called a kit or kitten.

# RADAR

SEE ALSO • Aeroplane • Airport • Boat • Invention • Radio

**Radar is a machine that sends out radio signals for tracking objects. The radio signals bounce off land and objects. Radar can work in the dark, in fog and over long distances.**

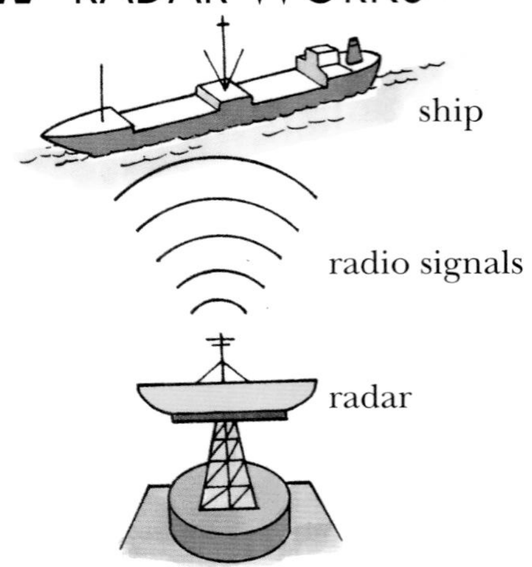


1. Radar sends out high-powered signals of radio energy.

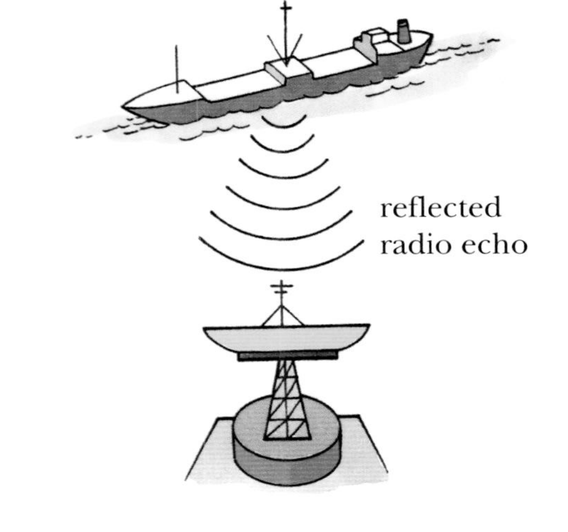


2. When a signal hits an object, a faint echo is sent back.

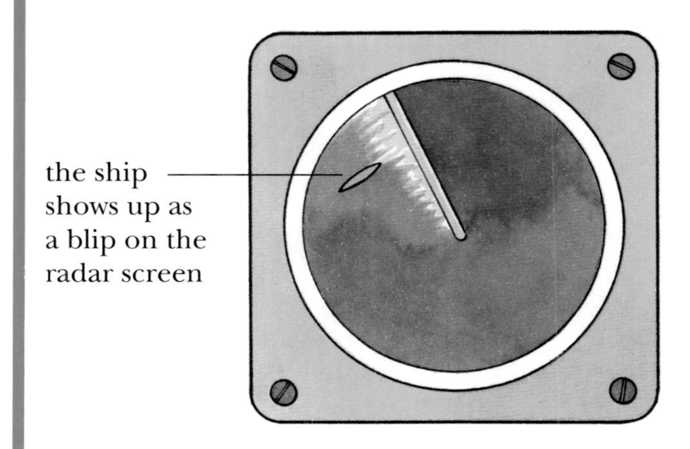


3. The echo is picked up by an antenna and shown as a blip on the radar screen.

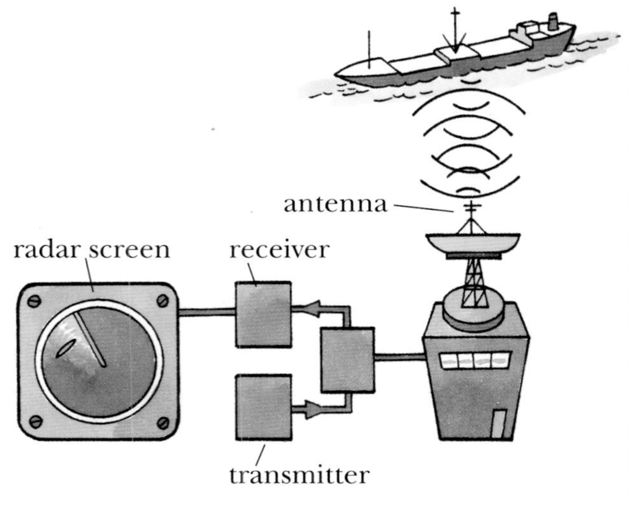


4. The direction in which the antenna is pointing gives the direction of the object.

## USES OF RADAR

- Ships use radar to navigate in fog.

- Police use radar to measure the speed of passing cars.

- Radar is used to show the exact position of an aeroplane.

- Weather stations use radar to follow storms.

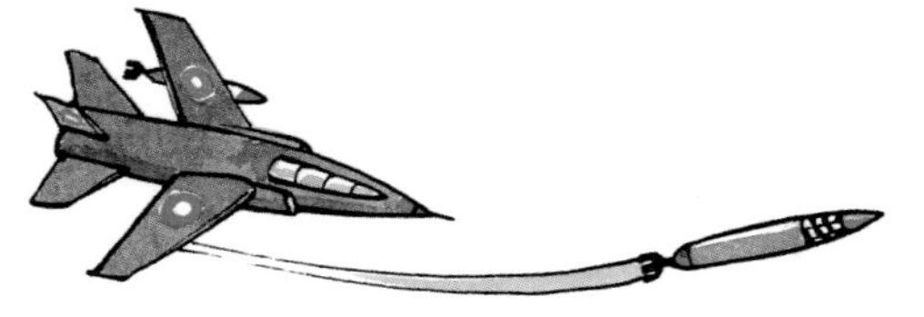

- Radar is used to detect and control missiles.

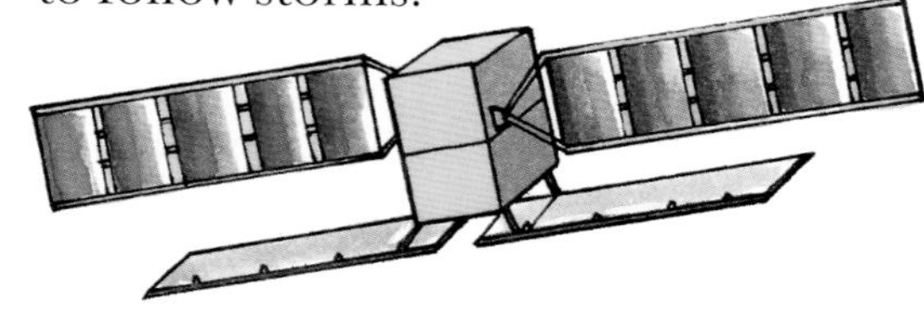

- Satellites fitted with radar are used to map the ground.

## RADAR OPERATORS ▼

Radar measures the delay between the time the signals are sent and the echo received. This tells operators how far away an object is.

## POLICE

Police use radar to catch motorists who are driving too fast.

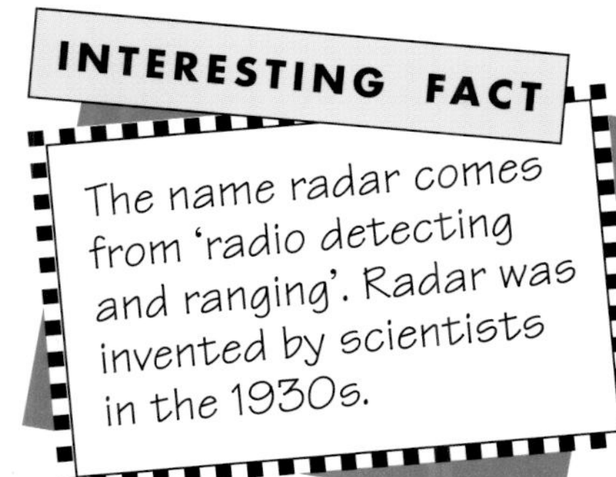

**INTERESTING FACT**

The name radar comes from 'radio detecting and ranging'. Radar was invented by scientists in the 1930s.

# RADIO

SEE ALSO • Invention • Radar

A radio is a machine that receives radio waves. Radio programmes are sent on radio waves all around the world. We can hear conversations, stories, plays, information programmes and all kinds of music on radio.

## HOW RADIO WORKS

1. A person speaks into a microphone. The microphone changes the sound into electrical signals.

2. The electrical signals are changed into radio waves.

3. The broadcasting antenna transmits the radio waves through the air.

4. An aerial on a radio picks up the radio waves. The radio changes the radio waves into the sound of the person speaking.

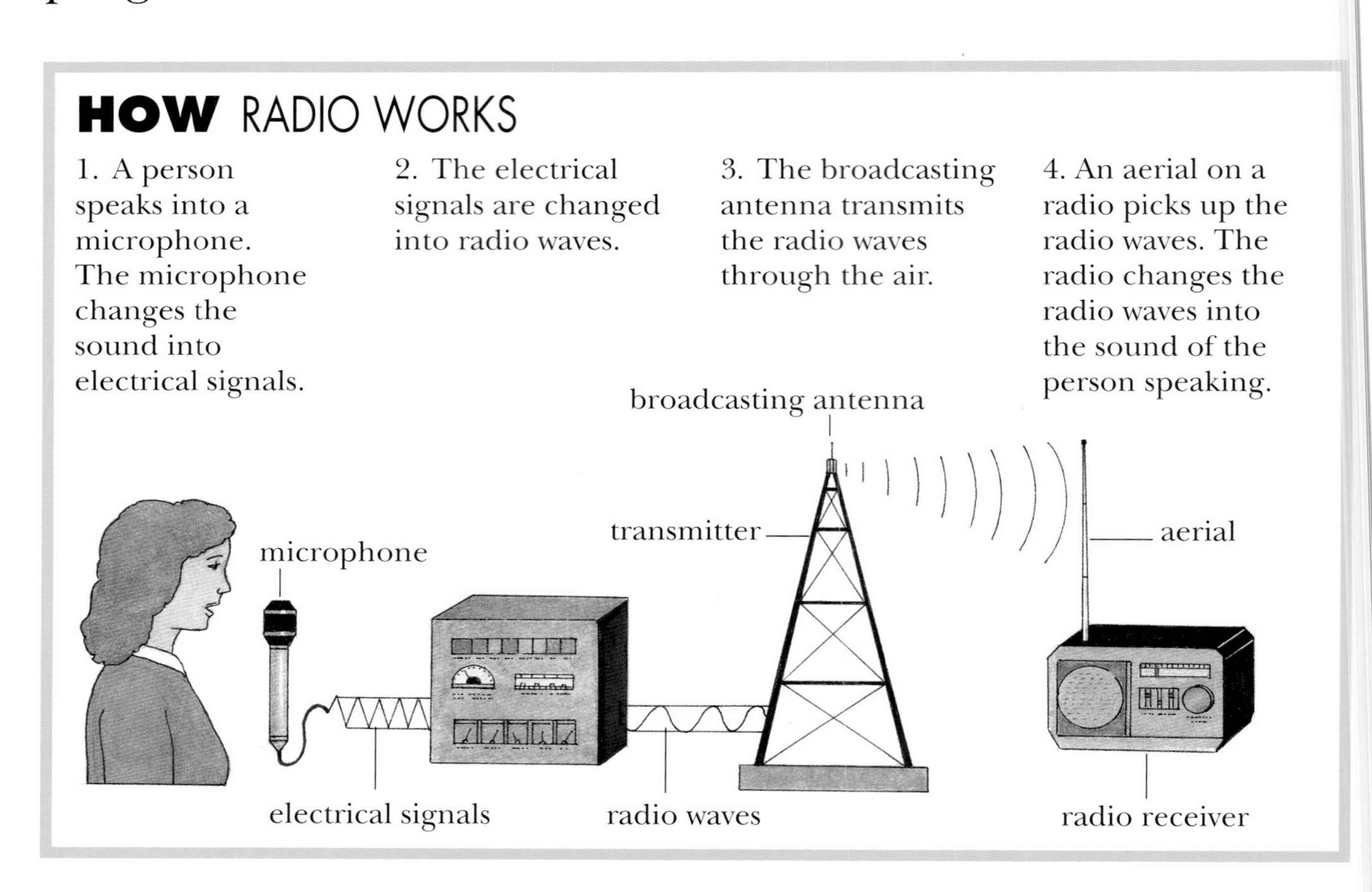

## HISTORY

From the 1920s until the 1940s, people listened to radio programmes in the same way that people watch television programmes today.

## USES OF RADIO

- Radio is used to broadcast radio programmes.
- Two-way radio is used by taxi drivers, ship captains, police and aircraft pilots to communicate.

### SCHOOL OF THE AIR

In many countries, children cannot attend school because it is too far away. They can talk to their teacher and other students over the radio.

### COMMUNICATION IN AEROPLANES ▲

A pilot radios the control tower for information about weather along the flight route.

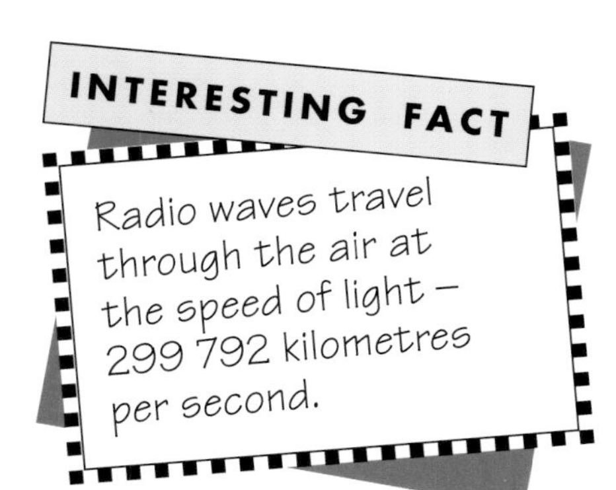


### A WIRELESS ▶

Radios send and receive sound without using wires. The first radio was called a wireless.

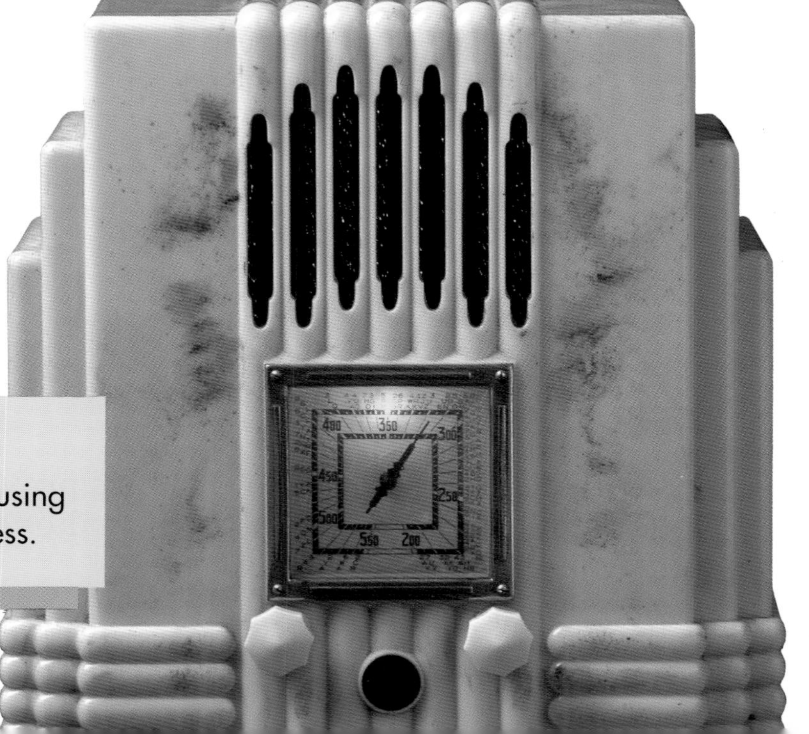

# RAIN

SEE ALSO • Cloud • Dam • Flood • Rainbow • Water • We ather

Rain is water that falls from the sky. A rain cloud is made up of millions of floating water droplets. When the droplets are too heavy and large to float, they fall to the ground as rain.

## HOW RAIN IS FORMED

Rain is part of the water cycle. Water moves in a cycle from the Earth to the atmosphere and back again.

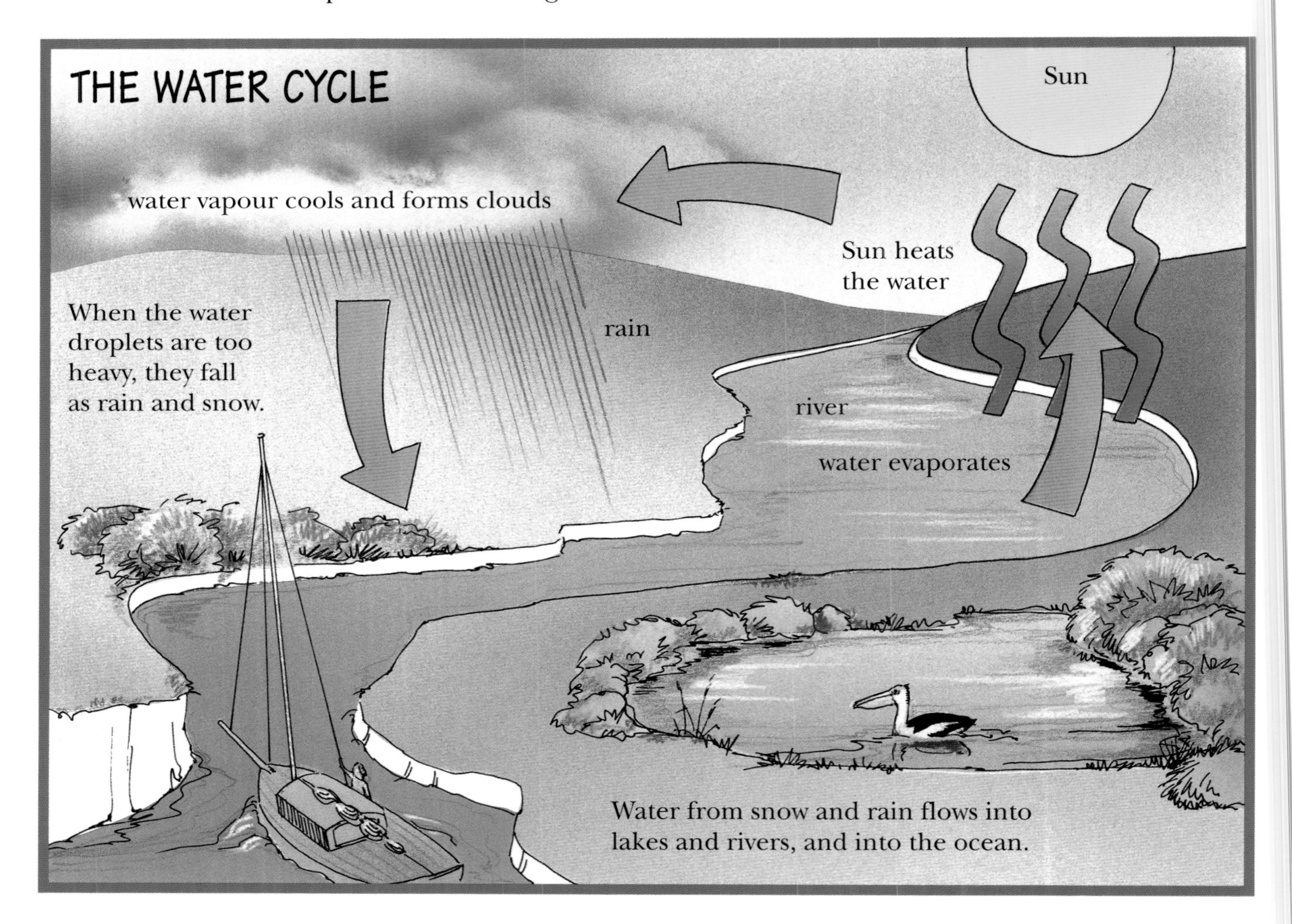


Plants need water to grow. Plants provide food for animals and people. Rain fills rivers and lakes with water which people and animals use to drink.

## SNOW

In very cold weather, the water droplets in clouds freeze to form crystals. Crystals stick together and form snowflakes. These fall to the ground as snow.

## SNOWFLAKES

Snowflakes are made of six-sided ice crystals. Every snowflake is different.

### INTERESTING FACT

Kauai in Hawaii, USA, has the most rainy days. Rain falls nearly every day of the year.

## MONSOON RAINS ▶

Monsoon rains are heavy rains. They fall in countries near the equator where it is hot all year. Farmers depend on the monsoon rains to grow their crops.

### INTERESTING FACT

Raindrops are round, not tear-shaped. They may vary from 0.5 millimetres to just over 5 millimetres in diameter.

# RAINBOW

SEE ALSO • Colour • Light • Rai

## A rainbow is the half circle of colours you can sometimes see in the sky. Rainbows appear when the Sun is shining through a shower of rain.

### HOW A RAINBOW IS MADE

A rainbow is made by sunlight shining on raindrops. Sunlight looks white but it is made of red, orange, yellow, green, blue, indigo and violet light.

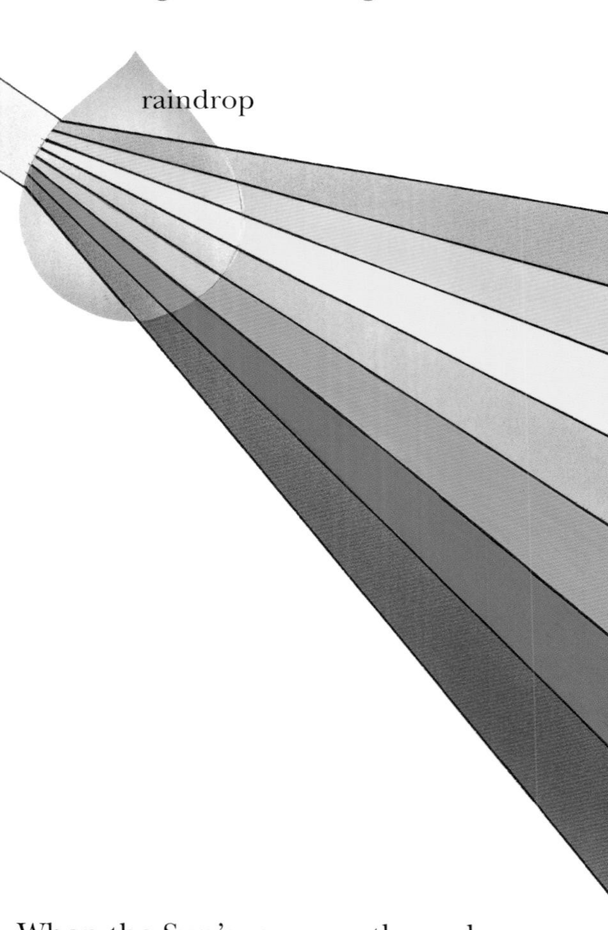


When the Sun's rays pass through millions of raindrops, the sunlight is separated into different colours and a rainbow forms.

Rainbows are really a full circle. On the Earth's surface, you can only see half a rainbow.

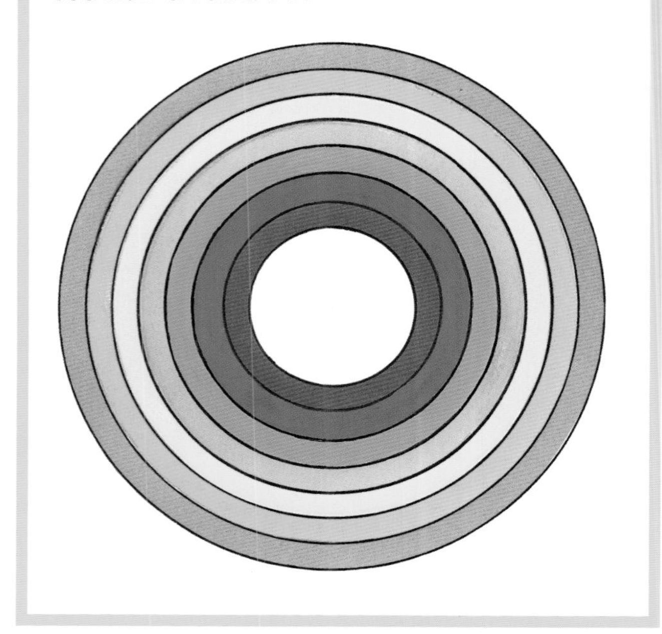

### A RAINBOW ▶

You may see a rainbow in the sky after a shower of rain. Look towards the sky with your back to the Sun.

## **COLOURS** OF A RAINBOW

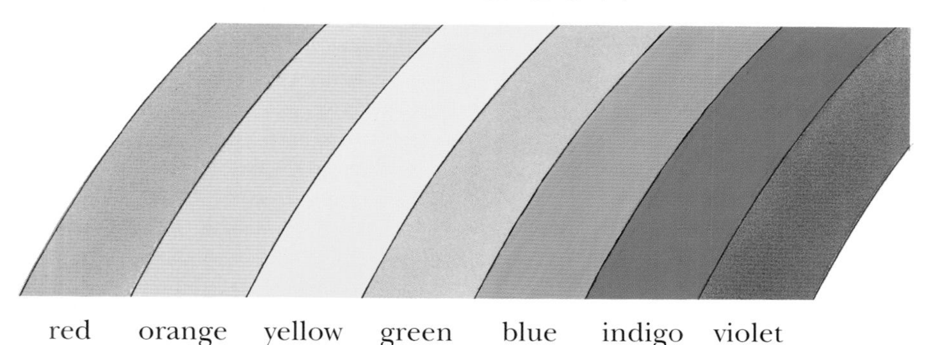


- A rainbow is made up of seven colours – red, orange, yellow, green, blue, indigo and violet.
- The colours are always in the same order.
- Usually, these colours mix with one another and you can only see four or five colours clearly.
- The amount of space each band of colour has changes. It depends on the size of the raindrops.

Rainbows can be seen in soap bubbles, crystals, diamonds, glass beads and in water spray from a hose or sprinkler.

**INTERESTING FACT**

High up in an aeroplane or standing on a high hill with the Sun behind you, you might be able to see a rainbow as a complete circle.

If a prism is in front of a beam of sunlight, it can separate all the colours in white light and make a rainbow.

▼

# RAIN FOREST

SEE ALSO • Earth • Ecology • Forest
• Plant • Tree

A rain forest is a kind of forest. Rain forests grow in places where it is hot and the rainfall is heavy. They provide a home for many different kinds of wildlife and plants.

## CONSERVING THE RAIN FORESTS

Rain forests are cleared to provide timber and to make way for crops, cattle and mining. Today, many countries are working together to protect our rain forests.

## LAYERS IN A RAIN FOREST

Different animals, birds, reptiles and insects live in different layers of a South American rain forest. Leopards, jaguars, snakes, frogs and other animals move between the layers of a rain forest.

**Emergent layer**
The tallest trees in the forest grow in this layer.

**Canopy**
The thick leaves form a cover like an umbrella. Little sunlight passes through the canopy.

**Undergrowth**
Plants such as vines, creepers, shrubs, palms and ferns grow in the dim light of this layer.

**Forest floor**
On the forest floor, dead plants rot quickly in the warm, humid weather. Insects and fungi break down the fallen leaves and wood which become part of the soil.

howler monkey

paradise tree snake

tree frog

cock-of-the-rock

## WHERE RAIN FORESTS ARE FOUND

● Africa
■ India
★ South East Asia
▲ Australia
◆ Central America
▼ South America

## MANGROVES

Mangrove swamps often grow where the rain forest meets the sea.

## FOREST PEOPLE ▲

Indian tribes live in the Amazon rain forest in South America. They live near the river or in small clearings. They have lived in the forest for thousands of years without destroying it.

# RAT

SEE ALSO • Animal • Mammal • Rodents

A rat belongs to the group of mammals called rodents. It is a furry animal with a long, thin tail. Black and brown rats are also called common rats.

## PARTS OF A BROWN RAT

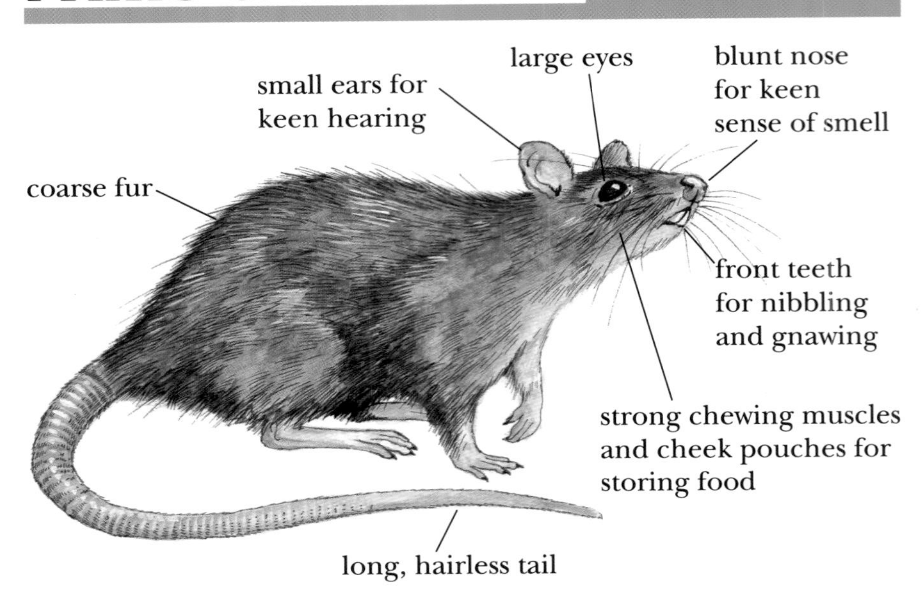


**Length:** 50 centimetres from nose to tip of tail (a rat's tail is as long as its body)

## FOOD

**Native rats**

seeds

grasses

insects

**Common rats**
plants and animals.

## WHERE RATS LIVE

Rats live in most parts of the world except the Antarctic.

## ◀ RATS AS PESTS

Black and brown rats are common in most parts of the world. They cause great damage to crops and buildings. They also spread diseases.

## MICE

Mice are closely related to rats. They are both rodents. Mice are much smaller than rats. There are many different kinds of mice.

- House mice are the most common.
- The harvest mouse is one of the smallest mice. It lives in the country. Harvest mice feed on corn and wheat stalks. They weave nests among the corn.

◄

## WATER-RATS

There are many different kinds of water-rats. They are found in many countries. Water-rats are well suited to life in the water. They have webbed hind feet and waterproof fur.

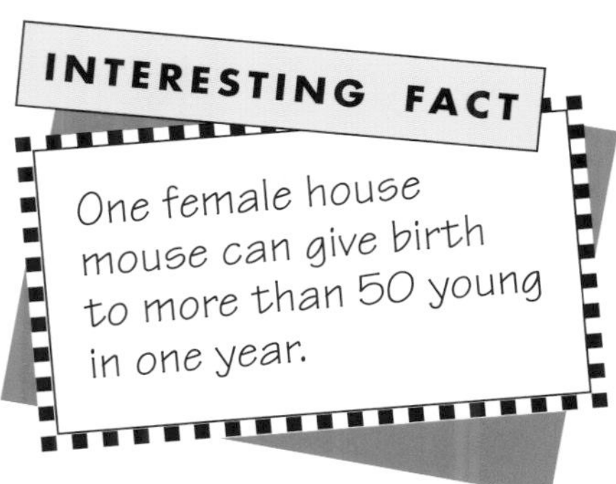

INTERESTING FACT

One female house mouse can give birth to more than 50 young in one year.

## HOW MICE AND RATS LIVE

- Mice and rats are born bald, blind and deaf. Within a few weeks, the young are covered with fur.
- After three weeks, the young have finished feeding on their mother's milk and are ready to explore.
- After six weeks, mice and rats start to breed.
- Rats and mice can have many litters each year.

# RECYCLING

SEE ALSO • Compost • Conservation

**Recycling is using things over and over again. It cuts down litter, reduces air and water pollution, and saves energy and resources.**

## LANDFILLS ▼

Most rubbish is taken to landfill sites.

## RECYCLING

Recycling paper, plastic, glass and metal helps to reduce rubbish.

- Glass bottles can be collected, cleaned and used many times.
- Recycling newspapers and other kinds of paper can save many hectares of trees.

- Recycling aluminium cans is easier and cheaper than processing aluminium from bauxite. ▶
- Recycled plastic is used to make many things.

## COMPOST

Compost recycles fruit and vegetable waste and garden rubbish.

# REFRIGERATOR

SEE ALSO • Invention • Machine • Electricity • Heat

A refrigerator keeps food and drink cold. Refrigerators are airtight to keep the cool air inside.

## HISTORY

Electric refrigerators were invented in the 1930s. Before then, fresh food was stored in cool places to keep it fresh. Ice was also used to keep food fresh.

## HOW A REFRIGERATOR WORKS

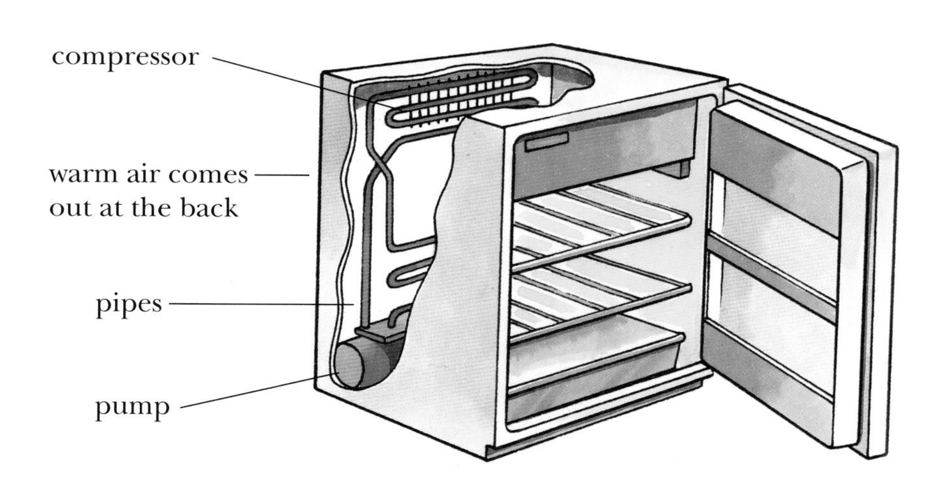


1. Inside the pipes is a liquid. The liquid turns to gas as it goes along the pipes, taking the heat away from the food in the refrigerator.

2. The gas goes into the compressor. It is turned back into a liquid.

3. Now, the liquid is ready to go through the pipes again. It will change to gas as it takes away more heat from the food.

4. When the food and drink is cool enough, a thermostat switches the compressor off until it is needed again.

# REPTILES

SEE ALSO • Animal • Vertebrate

Reptiles are a group of animals that have dry, scaly skin. They are cold-blooded animals. Their body temperature changes as the air temperature changes around them.

## REPTILE GROUPS

There are six main groups of reptiles:

- lizards
- snakes
- worm lizards
- turtles and tortoises
- crocodiles and alligators
- tuataras.

### INTERESTING FACT

Reptiles are the most ancient of all animals. The first reptiles lived on Earth 300 million years ago.

### CROCODILIANS

Alligators, crocodiles, caimans and gavials are in the crocodilian group of reptiles. The saltwater crocodile is the largest reptile. It is found in the swamps and rivers of northern Australia and New Guinea. It can grow up to seven metres in length.

### ◀ THE TUATARA

The tuatara is the last survivor of a group of ancient reptiles. It lives in New Zealand.

## WHERE REPTILES LIVE

Reptiles live on every continent except the Antarctic. They live in places where it is warm all the time. They need the heat from their surroundings to stay warm.

In cooler places, reptiles such as tortoises and snakes hibernate in winter.

## WORM LIZARDS

Worm lizards are almost blind. They find their prey such as insects, worms and rodents by smell and sound.

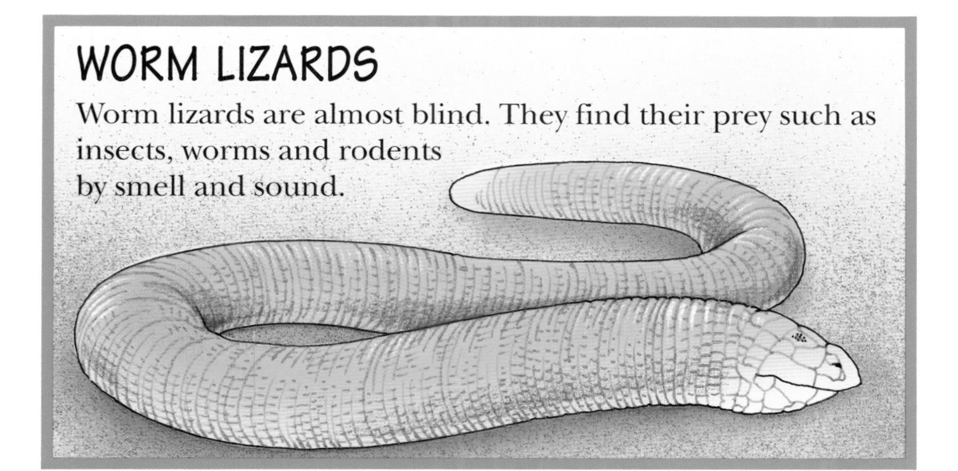

## LIZARDS ▼

Lizards are the biggest group of reptiles.

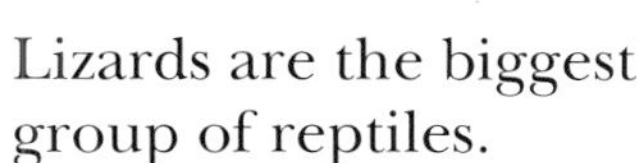

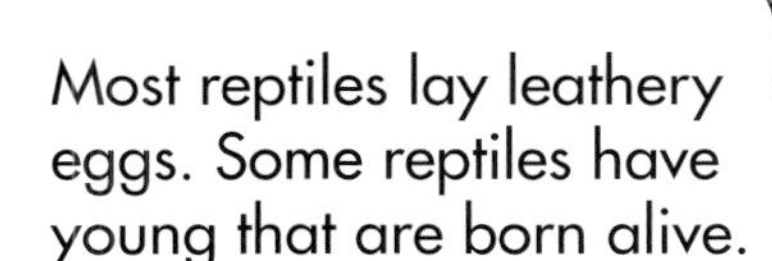

Most reptiles lay leathery eggs. Some reptiles have young that are born alive.

## TURTLES AND TORTOISES

Turtles, tortoises and terrapins are the only reptiles with shells.

## SNAKES ▼

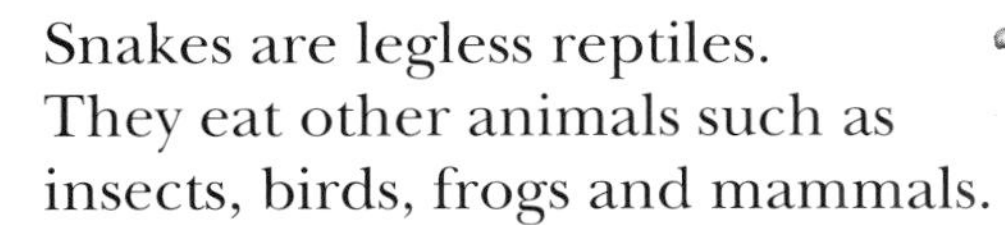

Snakes are legless reptiles. They eat other animals such as insects, birds, frogs and mammals.

# RHINOCEROS

SEE ALSO • Animal • Endangered Species • Mammal • Ungulates

A rhinoceros is a mammal. It is a large animal with thick skin that looks like armour. Rhinoceroses have one or two horns on their snout.

## PARTS OF AN INDIAN RHINOCEROS

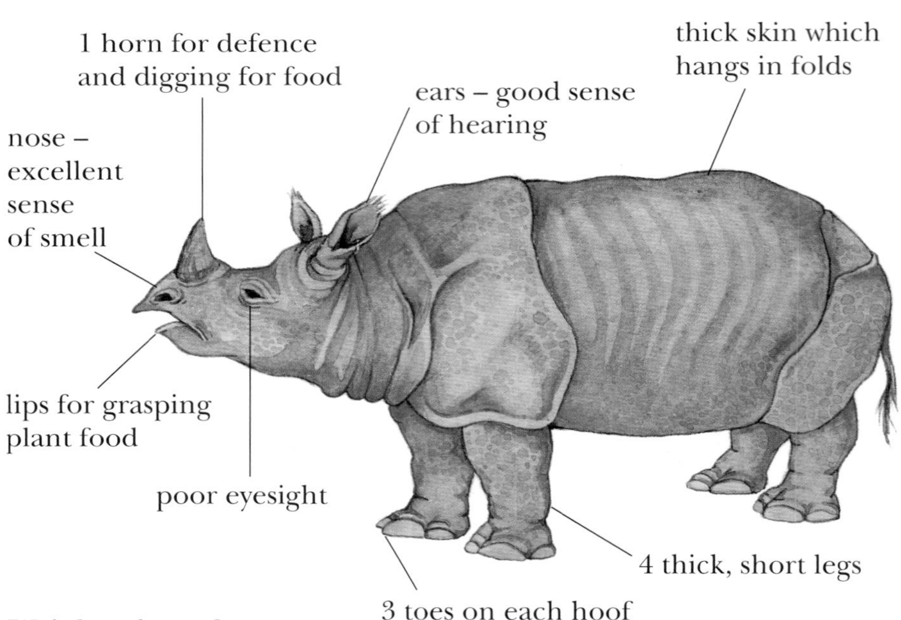


**Weight:** about 2 tonnes
**Height:** up to 2 metres

## FOOD

Rhinoceroses eat plants. They are herbivores.

## KINDS OF RHINOCEROSES

There are five kinds of rhinoceroses.

## INTERESTING FACT

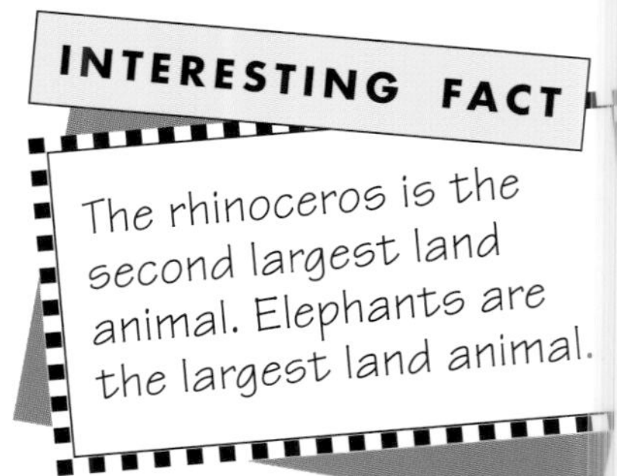

The rhinoceros is the second largest land animal. Elephants are the largest land animal.

## **WHERE** RHINOCEROSES LIVE

● Black and white rhinoceroses live on the African plains.

■ Indian, Javanese and Sumatran rhinoceroses live in the dense rain forests of Asia.

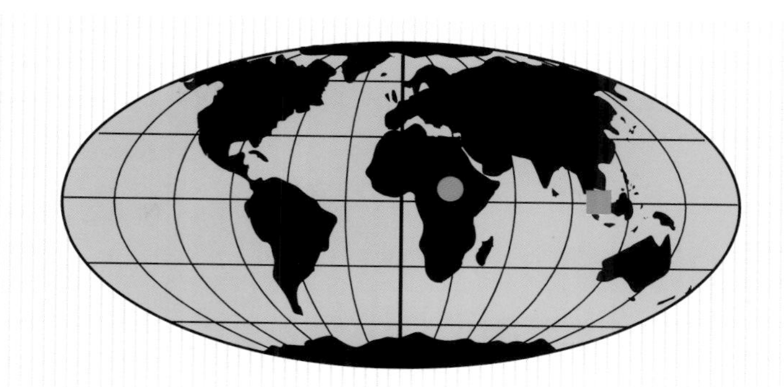

## **HOW** RHINOCEROSES LIVE

- Rhinoceroses usually live alone, except when mating and when their young are born.
- A female rhinoceros gives birth to one young at a time.
- The mother looks after the young rhinoceros until it can look after itself.

## ENDANGERED ANIMALS

Thousands of rhinoceroses have been hunted and killed for their horns. Today, rhinoceroses are protected animals.

## COOLING OFF 

Rhinoceroses cool off by wallowing in mud or water. Mud keeps their skin supple. When the mud dries, it drops off and removes skin parasites living on the rhinoceros.

## TAPIRS

Tapirs are closely related to rhinoceroses. They live in the forests of Malaysia and South America. They feed at night on plants on the open river banks. They spend the day in the water, eating river plants. Tapirs are in danger of losing their habitat because of forest clearing.

# RIVER

SEE ALSO • Flood • Glacier • Ocea[n] • Rain • Water • Waterfa[l]l

A river is a stream of water. Most rivers start high up in the mountains. Water from rain, melting snow and overflowing lakes runs down slopes. Rivers provide fresh water.

## RIVERS ARE USEFUL

- Rivers provide water to drink.
- Rivers provide water to irrigate plants.
- Rivers are used to transport people and goods.
- Rivers supply power for industry.
- Fish that live in rivers give us food.
- People use rivers for playing sports and having fun.
- Gold and quartz are found in some river beds.

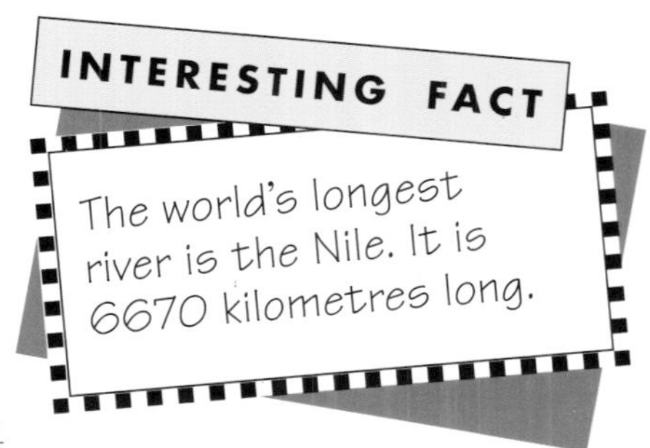


## A RIVER'S JOURNEY

**A river's course is the path of the river from the mountains to the sea. There are three parts in a river's course.**

source – this i
where a river egins

fast-running water

**The upper course**
Small streams start high up in the mountains. A stream picks up sand, gravel and rocks as it moves along.

tributaries are the streams and rivers th
flow into a big river

**The middle course**
The river becomes heavy with rocks and silt, and slows down as the land becomes flat. It cuts a snake-like pattern (meander).

waterfall

**The lower course**
The river slows down and becomes wider. Rocks and sand are worn down into silt.

mouth (where the river meets the sea)

estuary

## CITIES

In the past, people settled along river banks.
Modern cities have grown up from these early settlements.

## RIVER TRANSPORT

In thick rain forests, rivers are often the only way to travel from one place to another.

## **RIVER** SPORTS

People can have lots of fun when they spend time on rivers.

## **RIVER** WILDLIFE

A river provides a home for many different kinds of animals and plants.

dragonfly  frog  diving beetle  fish

water-rat  duck  turtle  otter

# ROAD

SEE ALSO • Bridge • Map • Motor Car • Transport • Truck

A road or highway is a strip of land for cars and trucks to drive along. Some roads are dirt tracks. Others are great networks of highways.

## HISTORY

The Romans made long, straight roads of gravel and stones. Some of these roads are still used.

## MOTORWAYS

Motorways let the traffic flow smoothly. Flyovers and underpasses let vehicles pass from one road to another without holding up traffic.

## HOW ROADS ARE MADE

1. Bulldozers clear an area of land and make it even.

2. Drains are laid to carry water away.

3. The road is built in several layers.

4. Steamrollers squash down each layer to make it firm.

# ROBOT

SEE ALSO • Computer • Invention • Spacecraft

A robot is a machine that can carry out tasks. A computer controls a robot's actions.

### ROBOTS IN ▶ FACTORIES

Robotic arms are used in factories to do jobs such as painting and spraying, heavy lifting and loading.

### REMOTE-CONTROLLED ROBOTS

Robots are used to work in places such as space and nuclear power stations. These places are dangerous for humans. The robots are controlled by an operator from a safe distance.

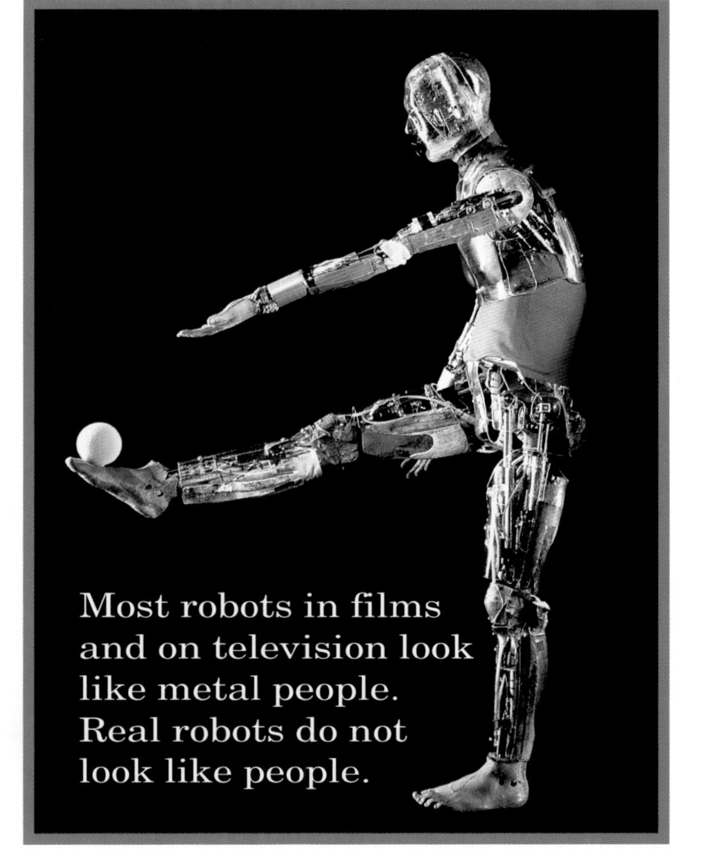

Most robots in films and on television look like metal people. Real robots do not look like people.

# ROCKS

SEE ALSO • Earth • Fossil • Minerals • Quarry • Volcano

Rocks are the hard part of the Earth's crust. Most rocks are covered by a layer of soil, grass or trees. All rocks contain materials called minerals.

You can see rocks in cliffs or areas where there is little soil or few plants growing.

Uluru in Australia is an enormous sandstone rock. It is 348 metres high.

## KINDS OF ROCKS

There are three main kinds of rocks – igneous, sedimentary and metamorphic.

**Igneous rock**
Deep inside the Earth, it is so hot that some rock is melted. This is molten rock. When molten rock cools and hardens, it forms igneous rock.

- Molten rock can cool below the Earth's surface.
- Some molten rock cools when it comes to the Earth's surface as lava.

Magma slowly cools underground and forms granite, an igneous rock.

**Sedimentary rock**

- Some sedimentary rocks are made from pieces of rock which are squashed and changed under the Earth's surface.
- Other sedimentary rocks are made from layers of dead animals and plants. The layers have hardened over millions of years.

Monument Valley in the USA is famous for its sandstone rocks. Sandstone is a sedimentary rock.

**Metamorphic rock**

- Metamorphic rock is made deep underground. Heat and pressure change sedimentary and igneous rocks into other kinds of rock. These are called metamorphic rocks.

Marble is a metamorphic rock. It is often used in buildings or by sculptors.

## SOIL

Soil is made from crumbled rocks.

1. Over millions of years, wind and water break rocks into tiny pieces.

2. The pieces of rock are mixed with decayed vegetable and animal matter called humus.

3. Bacteria, fungi and insects break down the humus. Insects and worms dig tunnels in the soil, making space for air and water.

# RODENTS

SEE ALSO • Animal • Dam • Guinea Pig • Mammal • Rat

Rodents are a large group of mammals. They have two top and two bottom teeth specially suited for gnawing. There are many different kinds of rodents which include mice, rats, porcupines and squirrels.

## WHERE RODENTS LIVE

Rodents live in most parts of the world except the Arctic and the Antarctic.

## FOOD

Most rodents are plant-eaters (herbivores). Some rodents such as rats eat other animals. They are carnivores.

bark roots grass nuts

## ENEMIES

Rodents have many enemies. Cats, foxes, birds, snakes and weasels hunt and eat rodents.

## GROOMING

When rodents groom their fur, they spread body oils which keep their fur untangled, free from pests and waterproof.

## KINDS OF RODENTS

Chipmunks live on the ground. They belong to the squirrel family. They hold their food in their front paws and use their teeth to crack nuts.

Lemmings are small, squat rodents. They have a blunt nose, a short tail and thick fur

The European beaver is well suited to life in the water. It has webbed feet, waterproof fur and a tail which acts like a rudder. Beavers build dams in the water with twigs and mud. They use their strong gnawing teeth to cut down trees.

▲
In deserts, gerbils line their nests with shredded plants.

The jerboa uses its long back legs to leap from place to place. It is active at night. During the day, it hides underground in burrows. ▼

The flying squirrel has flaps of skin between its front and back legs. It can glide from one tree to another.

The capybara is the largest rodent. It grows up to 1.25 metres long and weighs 45 kilograms. It lives in the forests of South America. It lives on the green parts of plants.

▼

# RUGBY

SEE ALSO • Football • Soccer

**Rugby is a kind of football which is played with two teams. You play Rugby by kicking, passing or running with the ball. Rugby started from a football game in England in the 1820s.**

## KINDS OF RUGBY

There are two kinds of rugby.

- Rugby Union has two teams of 15 players.
- Rugby League has two teams of 13 players.

The rules and scoring are different for each game.

A Rugby League pitch is a rectangle. It is usually 100 metres long and 68.62 metres wide. H-shaped goals are on the goal lines.

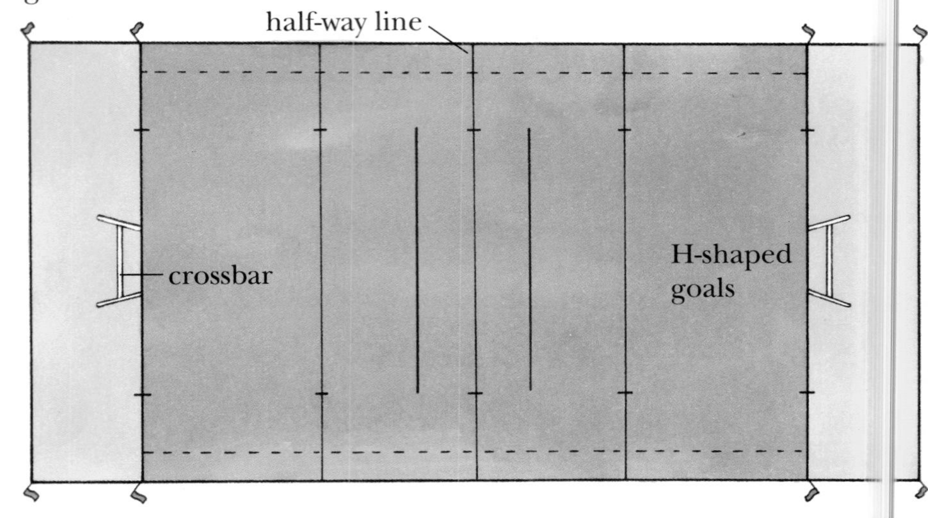


## SCORING

- A player scores a try when he puts the ball down over the other team's goal line.
- A player can score a goal by kicking the ball over the crossbar of the other team's H-shaped goal.

**SCRUMS ▶**

In Rugby, teams battle for the ball in scrums.

## LINE-OUT ▲

In Rugby Union, a line-out starts play after the ball has gone over the sidelines.

## REFEREES ▼

Rugby is a very fast game. A referee controls the game and keeps the score.

## TIME OF GAME

Usually 2 halves of 40 minutes.

# SAILING

SEE ALSO
• Boat • Floating • Kno
• Yacht • Water Sports

Sailing is a water sport. A sailing boat is moved along by wind in its sails.

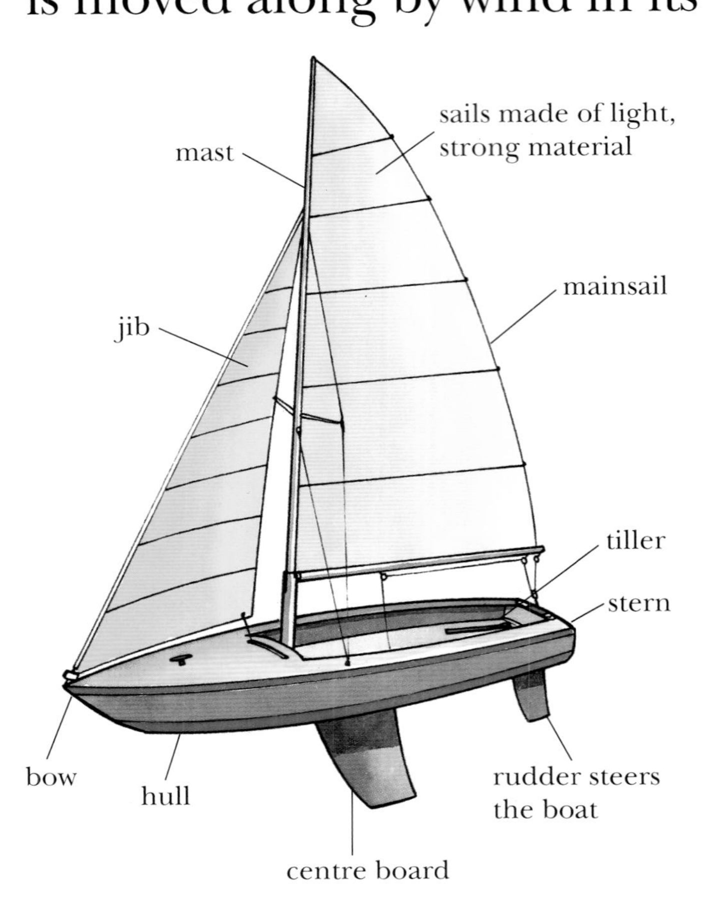


## TACKING

Sailing boats move easily with the wind. To move against the wind, you must sail a zigzag course. This is called tacking.

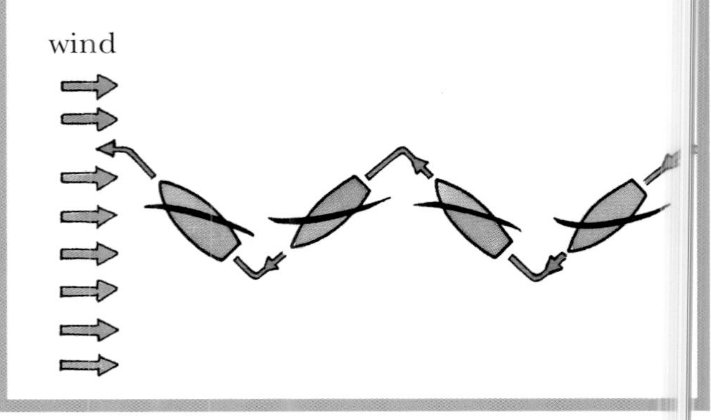


## SAILING SAFETY

- Wear a life jacket.
- Have a bucket for bailing water.
- Take a paddle in case the wind drops.

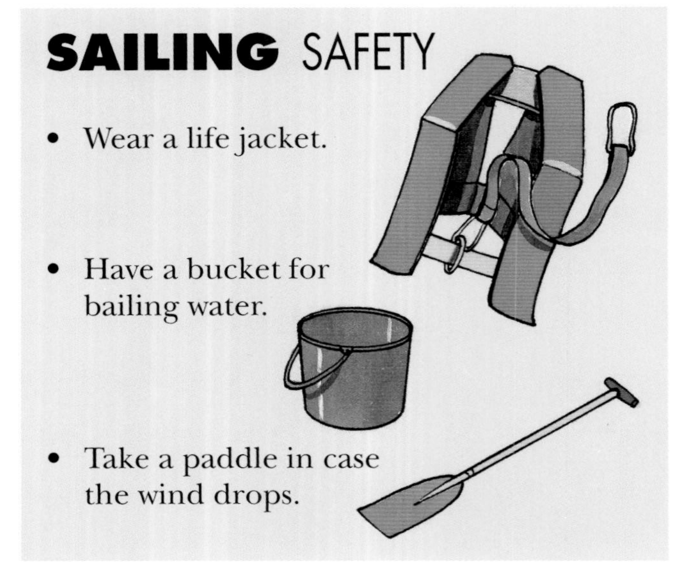

## SAILING TERMS

forward or fore – front
aft – back
galley – kitchen
starboard – the right-hand side of the boa
port – the left-hand side of the boat
spinnaker – an extra sail at the front

# SATELLITE

SEE ALSO • Astronaut • Moon • Planet • Spacecraft • Weather

A satellite is an object that orbits a planet. Some satellites are spacecraft. They are launched into space from the Earth and go into orbit around it.

## THE FIRST SATELLITE

The first satellite was Sputnik. It was launched by the Russians in 1957. It weighed 83 kilograms and carried a radio transmitter.

## KINDS OF SATELLITES

There are different kinds of satellites.

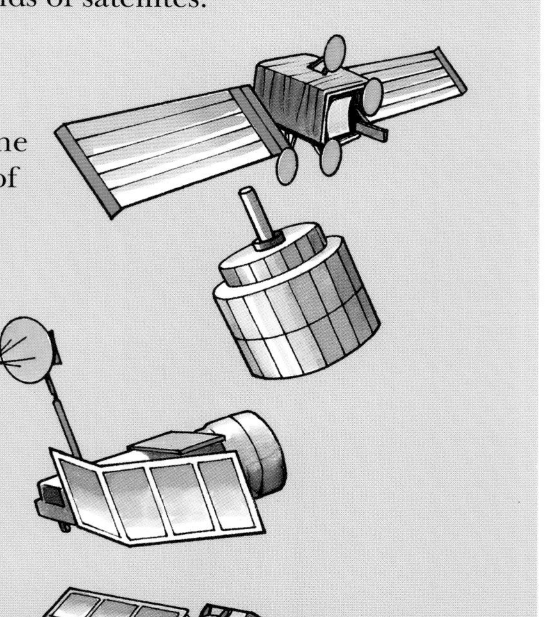

- Communications satellites send radio, television and telephone signals from one part of the Earth to another.
- Weather satellites observe the weather.
- Earth observation satellites monitor the environment.
- Navigational satellites are used by ships, aircraft and land vehicles to find their position.

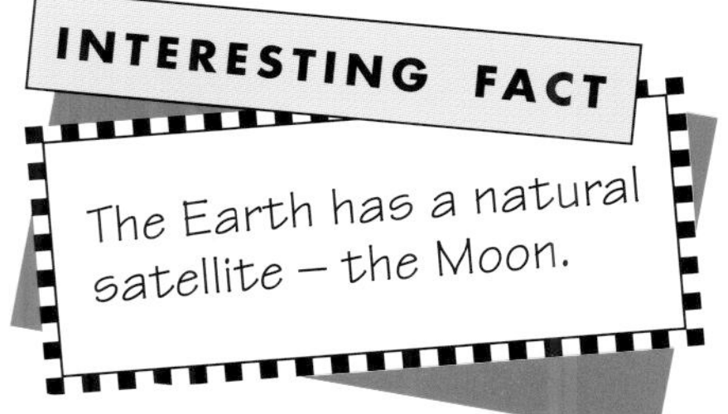


Satellites circle the Earth. They collect photographs and information about the Earth and space.

# SCHOOL

SEE ALSO • Book • Computer • Library • Paper • Printing

School is a place where children go to learn. Children learn from a teacher.

Most countries have three levels of school.

- Primary school is also called elementary school. It is the beginning of a child's school life. Children learn reading, writing, mathematics and other subjects.
- Secondary school is also called high school. Pupils study many different subjects.
- University and college are places where students can study after secondary school. They can study a subject that prepares them for a job.

## HISTORY

During the last one hundred years, schooling has become available for most people. Before that, only rich people went to school.

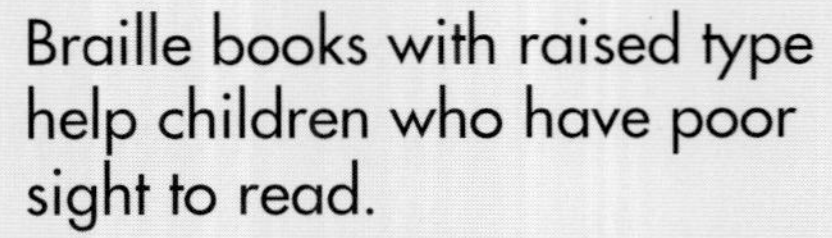

## SPECIAL SCHOOLS ▼

Braille books with raised type help children who have poor sight to read.

## SCHOOLS IN DEVELOPING COUNTRIES

In some countries, there is little money for building schools and providing equipment.

# SEAHORSE

SEE ALSO • Animal • Fish

A seahorse is a small fish. It has a head that looks like a horse's head and a long, curly tail. Seahorses live in most oceans.

## PARTS OF A SEAHORSE

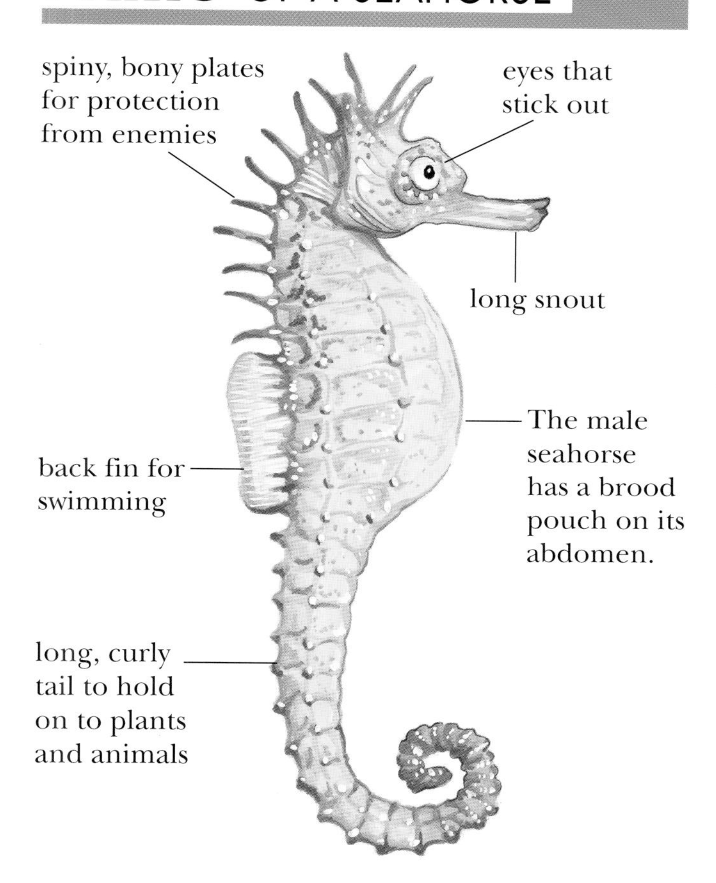


**Length:** 20 to 30 centimetres

## FOOD

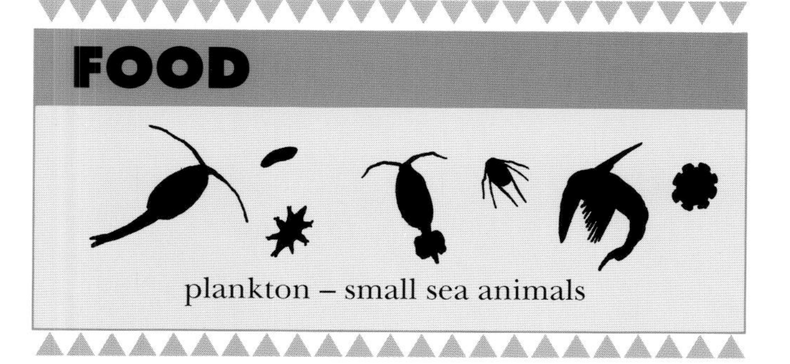

plankton – small sea animals

## HOW A SEAHORSE MOVES

A seahorse swims in an upright position. It waves its back fins.

## HOW SEAHORSES LIVE

Seahorses mate in spring and summer. The female seahorse lays hundreds of eggs in the brood pouch of the male seahorse. After about four weeks, the eggs hatch.

# SEAL

**SEE ALSO** • Animal • Antarctic • Arctic • Mammal

A seal is a large, furry mammal that lives in the sea. Seals are graceful swimmers. They swim ashore to breed.

## PARTS OF A HARBOUR (COMMON) SEAL

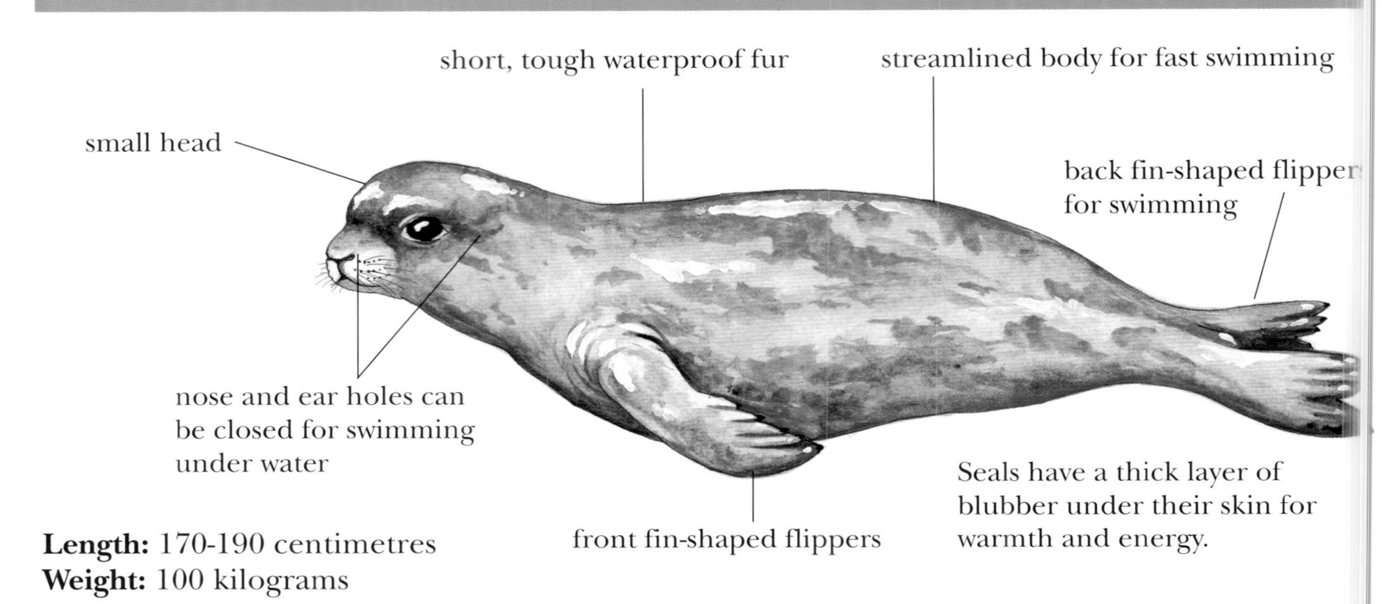


**Length:** 170-190 centimetres
**Weight:** 100 kilograms

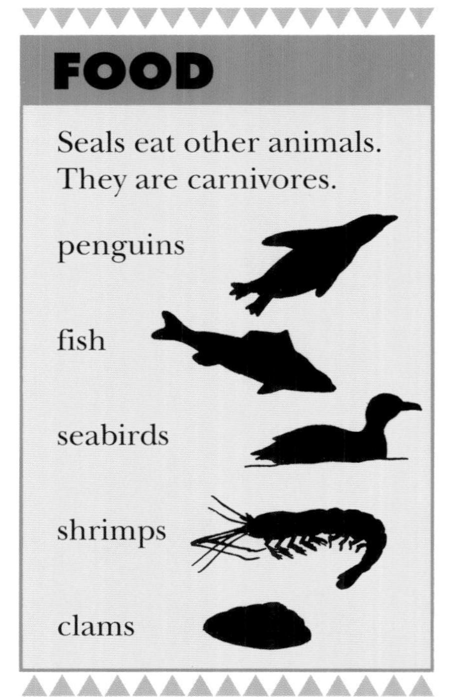

## FOOD

Seals eat other animals. They are carnivores.

penguins

fish

seabirds

shrimps

clams

## HOW SEALS LIVE

- Seals breed in spring and summer. They swim ashore and breed in large groups called colonies.
- Females usually give birth to one pup every year. The female seal feeds her pup with milk for several months. The pup may stay with the mother for up to two years.

## KINDS OF SEALS

- Eared seals include fur seals and sea lions.
- Earless seals have ear openings but no ears. Harbour seals, walruses and elephant seals are earless seals.

## HOW SEALS MOVE

- Earless seals swim by moving their bodies and rear flippers like fish. They pull themselves across land or ice.
- Fur seals, sea lions and walruses fold their front flippers under their bodies to rest on land. They walk on all four flippers.

### INTERESTING FACT

Seals shed their coats each year and grow a new one. They only shed a few hairs at a time like cats and dogs.

## ◀ SEA LIONS

Sea lions are eared seals.

## WHERE SEALS LIVE

Seals live along the coasts of continents. Most seals live in the Arctic and the Antarctic.

## WALRUSES

Walruses are closely related to seals. They have huge tusks. They use their teeth or tusks to cut breathing holes in the ice and to drag themselves on to the ice to rest.

## THE BIGGEST SEAL ▶

The elephant seal is the biggest seal. It can grow up to six metres long and weigh three tonnes.

# SEASHORE LIFE

SEE ALSO • Bird • Echinoderm • Ecology • Jellyfish • Molluscs

The seashore is where the land meets the sea. It provides a home for many living things.

## KINDS OF SEASHORE LIFE

Different kinds of living things live on different parts of the seashore. The seashore is always being changed by the waves and the tides going in and out.

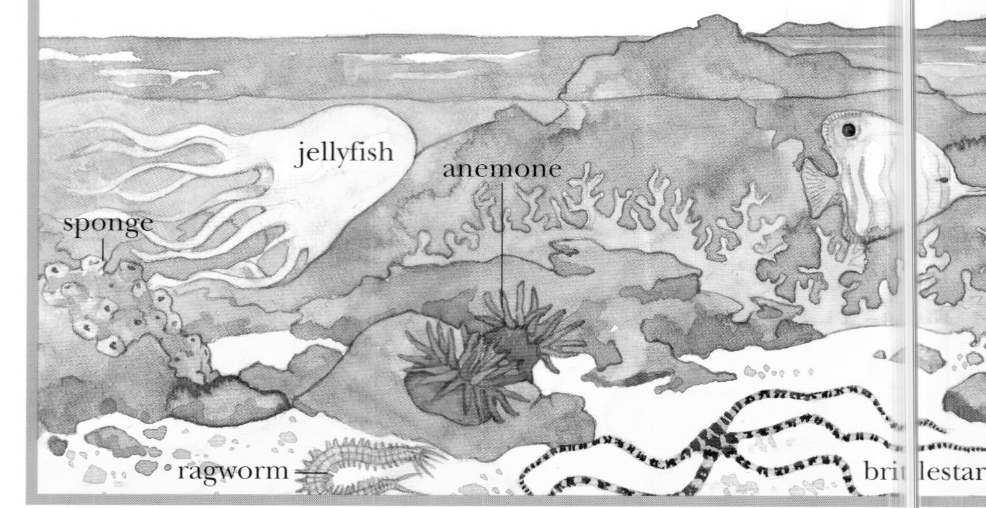


## DIFFERENT KINDS OF SEASHORE

## LIFE IN A ROCK POOL ▶

Many plants and animals cling to rocks in a rock pool. They eat tiny pieces of food that float in the water.

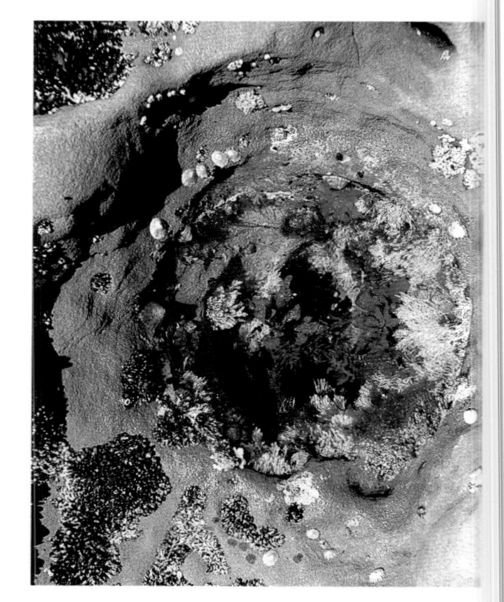

## ◀ SEAWEED

Seaweed is a plant that lives in the sea. It provides food and shelter for other living things.

## A SEASHORE ECOSYSTEM

All seashore animals and plants are linked together in different ways. Upsetting one kind of seashore life can change all the other seashore life.

## SEASHORE BIRDS

Many birds live along the shore.

- Some birds fish at sea.

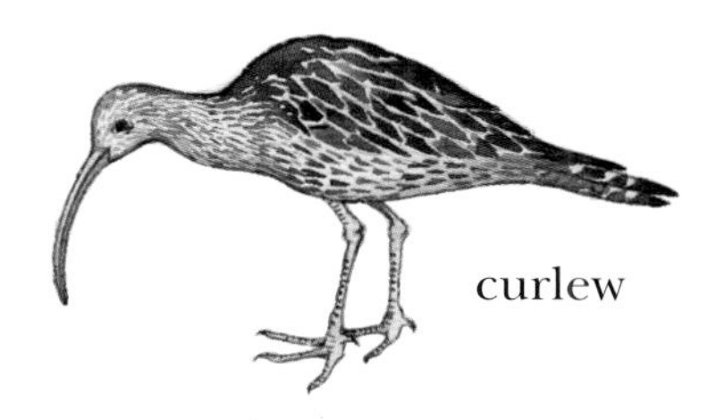


- Some birds use their long beaks to dig in the sand for worms and insects.

- Some feed on small bits of food brought to the shore by the tide.

### PUFFINS ▶

Birds such as puffins make nesting places on cliff ledges. A few plants and animals such as snakes also live on cliffs.

# SEASON

SEE ALSO • Calendar • Months of the Year • Weather

A season is a time of the year. There are four main seasons – spring, summer, autumn and winter. Seasons happen because of the way the Earth travels around (orbits) the Sun.

## HOW SEASONS HAPPEN

The Earth is tilted on its axis. It leans to one side.

As the Earth orbits the Sun, one half is closer to the Sun than the other. The part closest to the Sun has summer. The part furthest from the Sun has winter. As the Earth keeps moving around the Sun, the other half moves closer to the Sun. Now this part has summer.

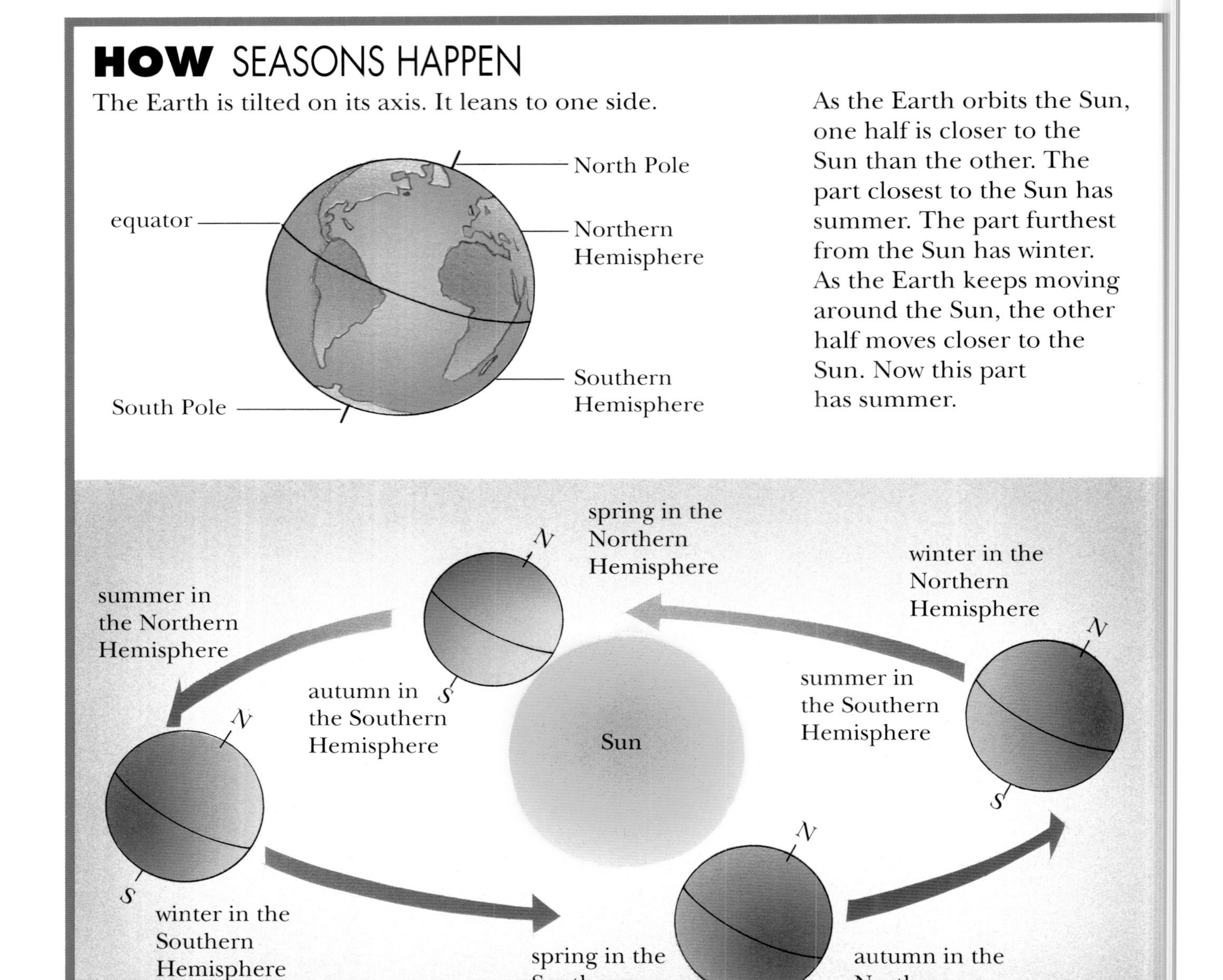

## SPRING

In spring, the days become warmer. Plants begin to grow. Young animals are born.

## SUMMER

Summer is the hot season. Plants bear fruit. Young animals grow.

## AUTUMN

In autumn, the days become cooler. The leaves fall from the trees. Animals store food for winter.

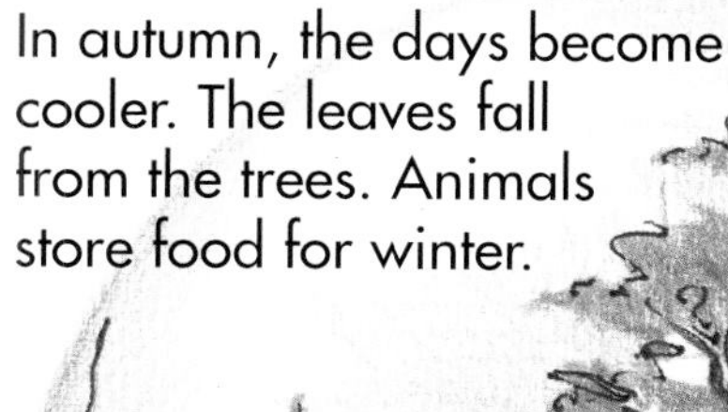

## WINTER

Winter is the cold season. Plants are dormant. Many animals hibernate.

**INTERESTING FACT**

At the poles, there are only two seasons, summer and winter.

## WET SEASON

At the equator, it is hot all year around. Countries near the equator have a wet season and a dry season.

# SHARK

SEE ALSO • Animal • Fish • Fishing

A shark is a large, fast-swimming fish. It does not have a skeleton of bones; it has a skeleton of gristle. Some sharks are fierce hunters.

## PARTS OF A SHARK

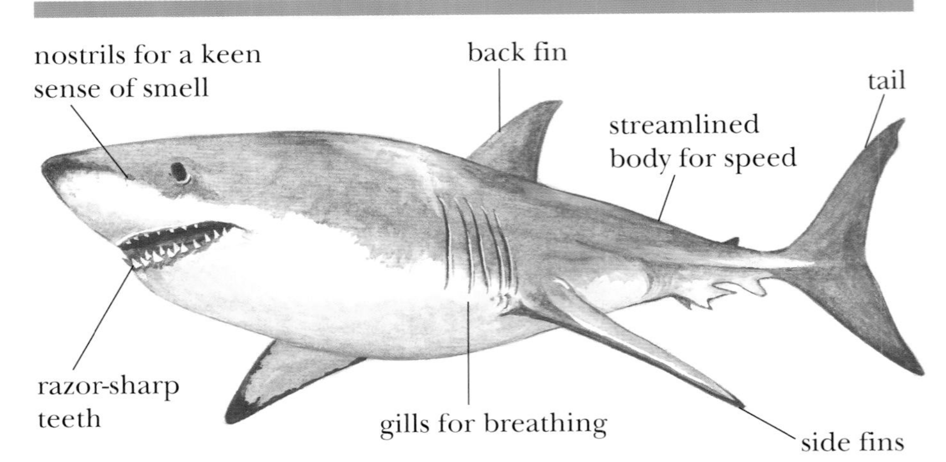


## WHERE SHARKS LIVE

Sharks live in oceans all over the world, but most are found in warm waters.

## INTERESTING FACT

Sharks have to swim all the time or they will sink. They do not have a swim bladder to help them float.

## SHARK TEETH

Sharks have rows of razor-sharp teeth. When one tooth is lost, another grows in its place.

## FOOD

Most sharks eat other sea animals. They are carnivores.

## KINDS OF SHARKS

There are many different kinds of sharks.

The great white shark is dangerous. It sometimes attacks people. ▼

The whale shark is the biggest fish in the sea. Although it is more than 15 metres long, it is harmless. It only eats plankton. ▶

◀ The spiny dogfish is the smallest shark. It is only 60 centimetres long.

A hammerhead shark has a head that looks like a hammer. ▼

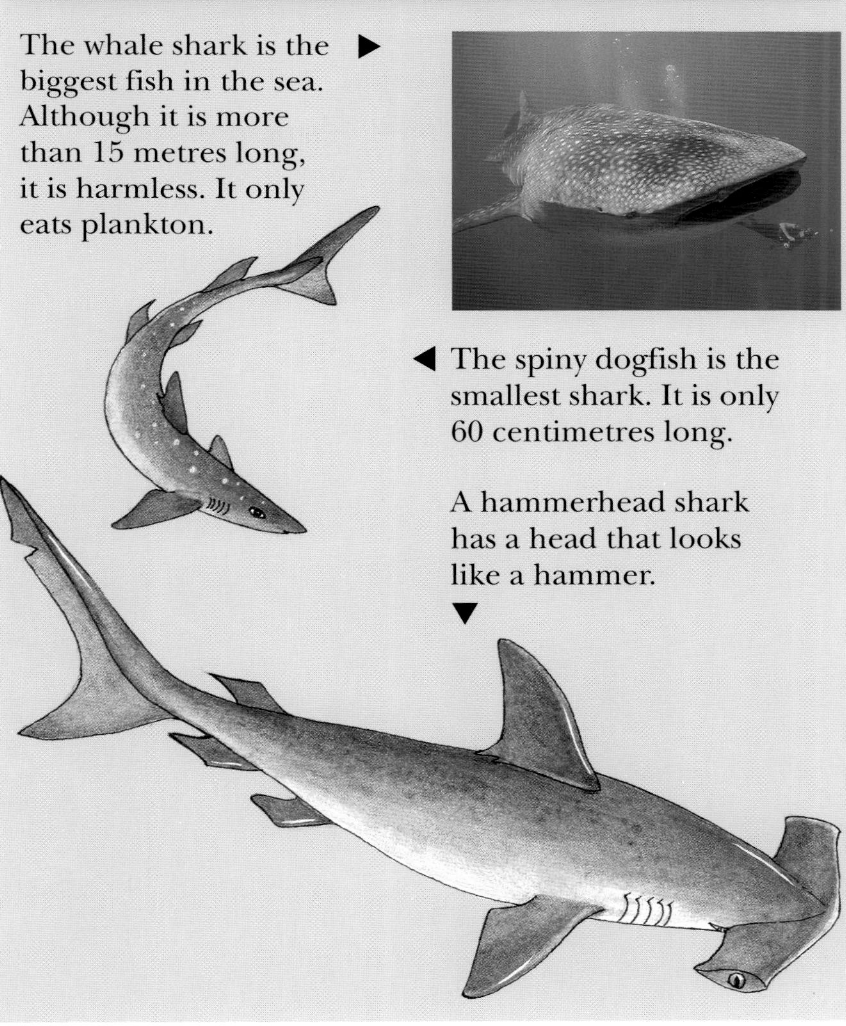

## HOW SHARKS LIVE

Different sharks breed in different ways.

- Some sharks lay eggs. The eggs hatch in 6 to 15 months.
- Some sharks develop inside their mother. The young pups are born fully developed after two years.
- Some sharks grow in eggs which hatch inside the mother's body.

### RAYS

Rays are close relatives of sharks. A stingray is one kind of ray. It has a sting at the end of its tail.

# SHIP

SEE ALSO • Boat • Floating • Satellit
• Submarine • Transport

A ship is a large boat.
Ships carry people and cargo across oceans from one country to another.

## PARTS OF A CARGO SHIP

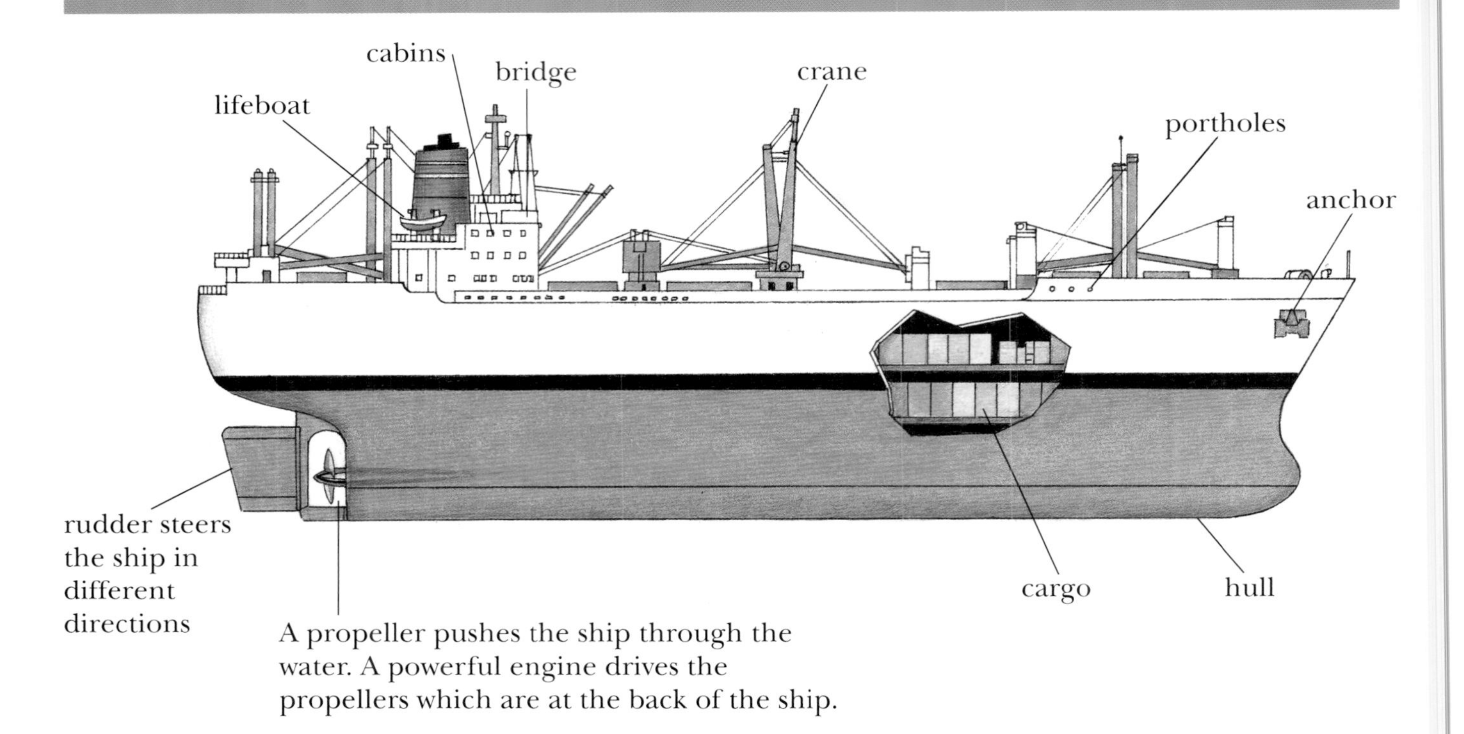


### COMMAND POST ▶

The captain commands the ship from the bridge. The steering wheel is on the bridge. Compasses, radar equipment, satellites, radio and charts are used to navigate the ship's course.

## HOW A SHIP FLOATS

Most ships are made of heavy metal.

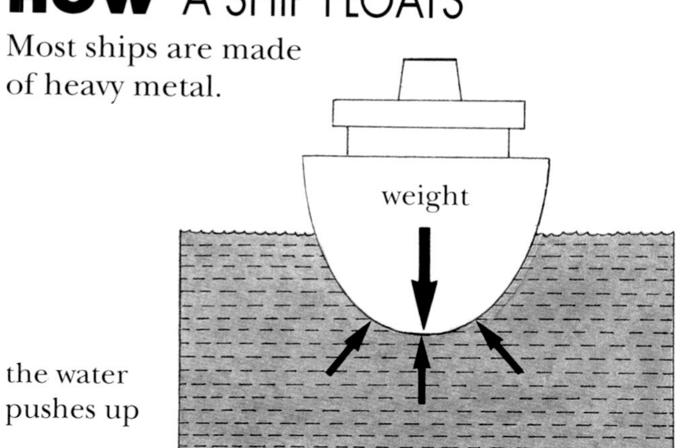


- The weight of the ship pushes the water out of the way.
- At the same time, the water pushes back. This is called upthrust.
- The upthrust balances the weight of the ship and keeps it afloat.

## HOW SHIPS BALANCE IN WATER

The bottom of a ship is shaped so that when it leans over it always becomes level again.

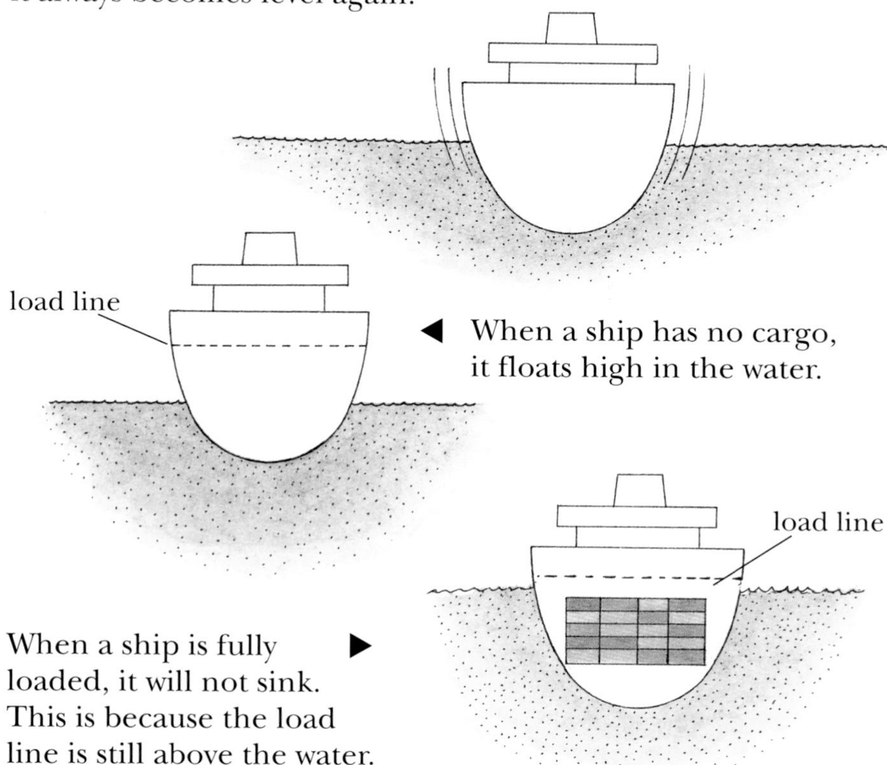


◀ When a ship has no cargo, it floats high in the water.

When a ship is fully loaded, it will not sink. This is because the load line is still above the water. ▶

## KINDS OF SHIPS

There are many different kinds of ships. Today, most ships are cargo ships.

Container ships can carry all sorts of goods packed into large containers.

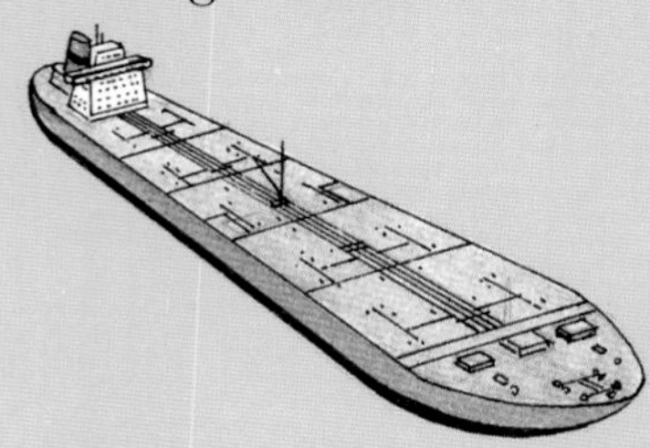

Oil tankers carry oil across oceans.

Ferries carry trucks, passengers and their cars across a stretch of water.

Ocean liners carry people who are on holiday.

# SHOP

SEE ALSO • Bank • Food • Money

A shop is a place where you can buy things. People exchange money for the things they need.

## HISTORY

Long ago, people used to swap the things they needed. This was called bartering.

## MODERN SHOPPING CENTRES

A shopping centre has many different shops in one area. Shopping centres also have car parks, restaurants and places to sit and rest.

## CASH REGISTERS

Cash registers or tills were invented in 1879. They record each sale and keep the money safe. Today, computerized registers add up the bill, print a receipt and keep records of stock.

## DEPARTMENT STORES

A department store is a large shop that sells many kinds of goods in separate sections.

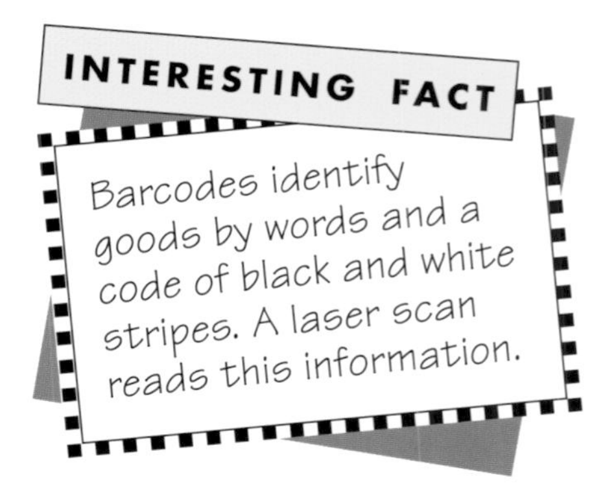

**INTERESTING FACT**

Barcodes identify goods by words and a code of black and white stripes. A laser scan reads this information.

# SKELETON

SEE ALSO • Human Body • Invertebrate • Vertebrate

A skeleton is made of bones. It supports an animal's body. In humans and other vertebrates, the skeleton is inside the body. An invertebrate's skeleton is outside its body.

## PARTS OF A SKELETON

A human skull is made up of 22 bones.

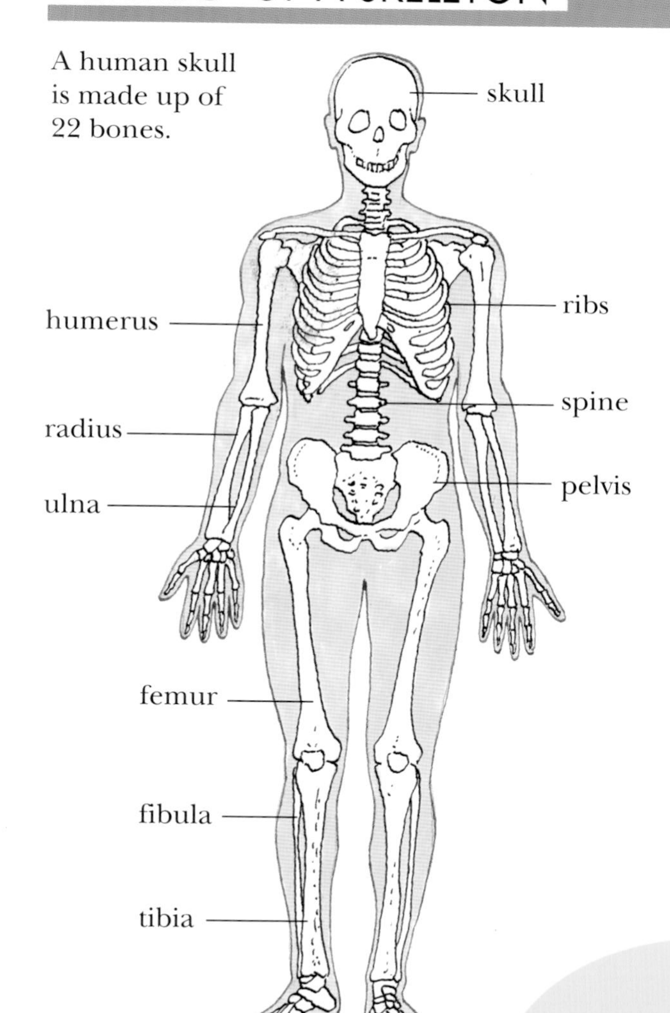


More than half of our bones are in our hands, feet and ankles. The longest bone is the thigh bone (femur).

Your skeleton is important.

- It supports and gives shape to your body.
- It helps to protect your organs.
- Minerals such as calcium are stored in your bones.
- Muscles and bones work together to help you move.

### HOW MANY BONES?

A baby is born with about 270 bones. As the baby grows, some bones separate and some grow together. An adult has only 206 bones.

### BROKEN BONES

If a bone cracks or breaks, it will heal if it is kept still.

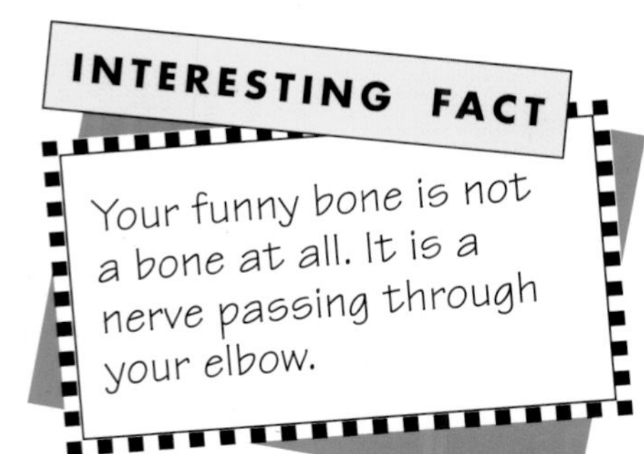

# SKIING

SEE ALSO
• Olympic Games
• Ice Skating • Water Sports

## Skiing is a sport. It is a way of travelling across snow. Skiers wear long, flat runners or skis on their feet.

There are different kinds of skiing:
- Nordic – cross-country and ski jumping
- alpine – skiing downhill
- freestyle – skiers perform stunts.

▲
Cross-country skiing has been the main way of getting about on deep snow for thousands of years. Today, it is a popular sport.

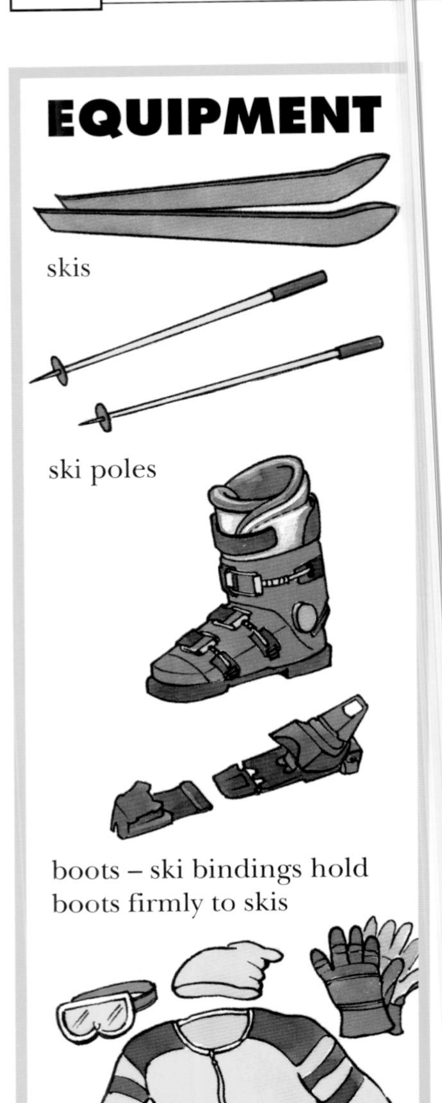

◀ WINTER OLYMPICS
Skiing competitions are popular at the Winter Olympics.

# SKIN

SEE ALSO • Blood • Hair • Human Body

Skin covers all of your body. It protects your body and helps to control your body temperature. Skin can feel shape, size, texture and temperature.

## PARTS OF THE SKIN

Skin has different layers.

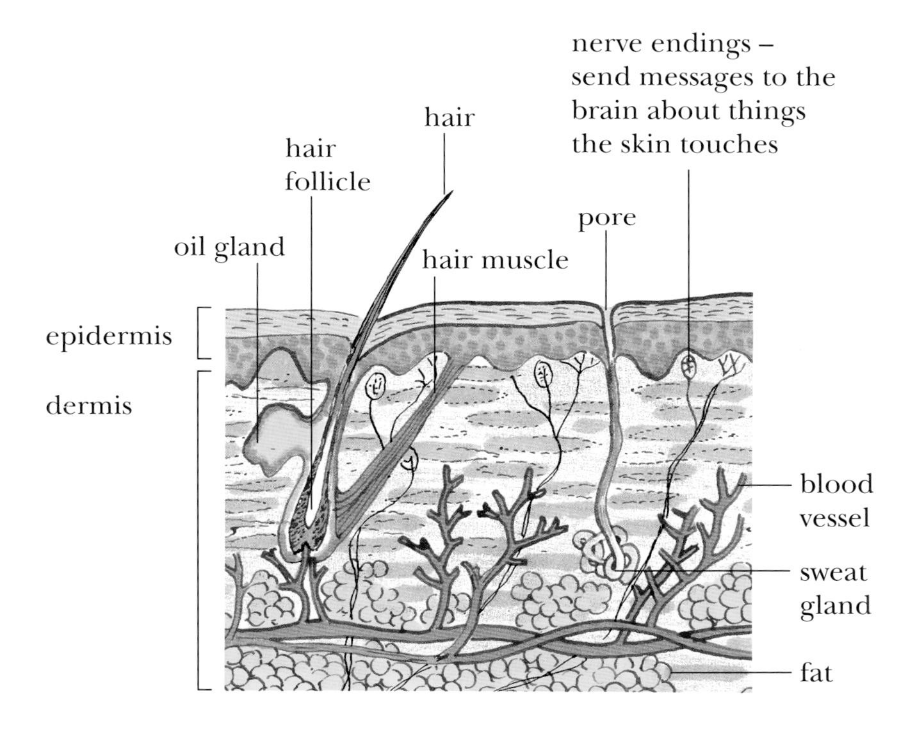


### PROTECTING YOUR SKIN FROM THE SUN ▼

The ultraviolet rays of the Sun destroy the cells of the epidermis. Cover your skin to protect it from the Sun.

## THE EPIDERMIS

The epidermis is the top layer. It grows all the time. It replaces dead cells which are rubbed off. The epidermis protects the sensitive lower layer, the dermis.

## THE DERMIS

The dermis is the second layer. It contains:

- nerve endings which feel pain, cold, heat and pressure
- oil glands
- sweat glands
- hair roots.

# SNAIL

SEE ALSO • Animal • Garden • Molluscs • Pond Life • Seashore Life

A snail is an animal with a soft body and a shell on its back. The shell protects its soft body. Snails belong to a group of animals called molluscs.

## PARTS OF A GARDEN SNAIL

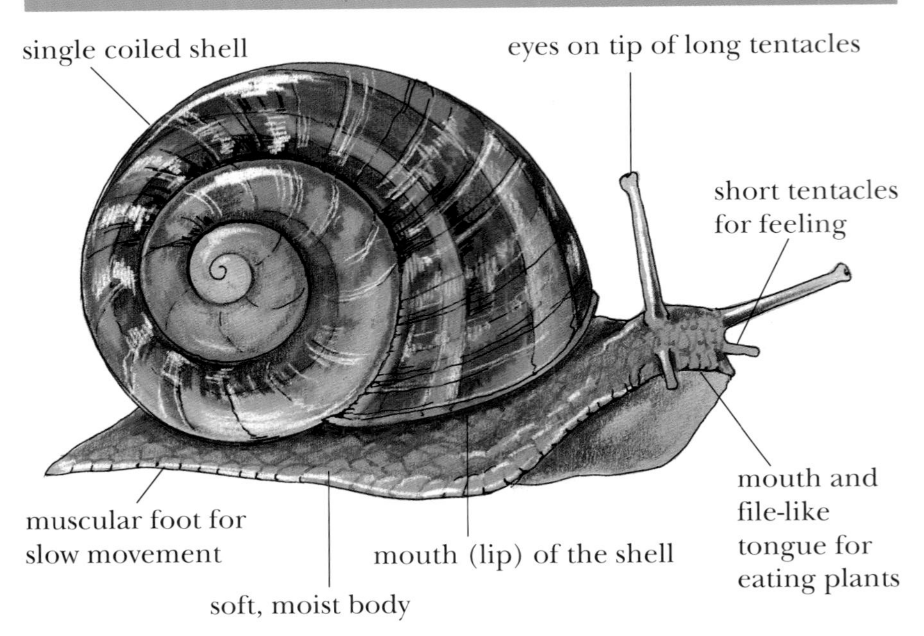


**Length:** 3 centimetres

## HOW GARDEN SNAILS LIVE

- After mating, snails lay small, rubbery eggs.
- The young snails hatch from their eggs after two to four weeks.
- Snails can live for 2 to 20 years.

## FOOD

Most snails eat living or dead plant material. Some snails eat small animals.

## A SNAIL'S SHELL

- A snail can withdraw inside its shell for protection.
- During hot, dry or cold weather, snails often sleep and seal their shell openings. This stops their soft bodies from drying out.
- As the snail grows, its shell also grows. It adds more material to the mouth of the shell.

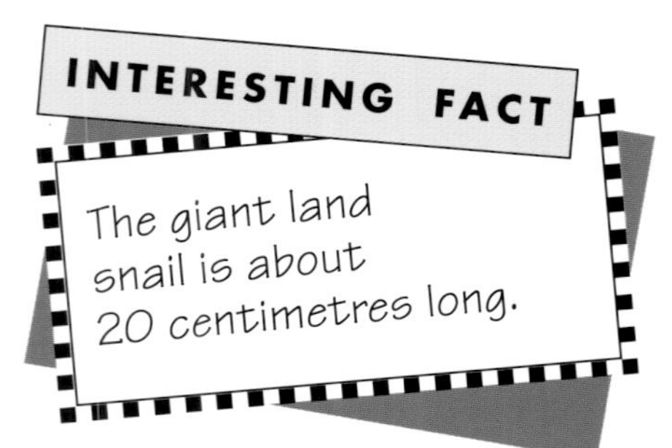

**INTERESTING FACT**

The giant land snail is about 20 centimetres long.

## LAND SNAILS

Land snails are found in damp, shady places. Most land snails have lungs.

## FRESHWATER SNAILS 

Freshwater snails are found in rivers, ponds, lakes and hot springs. Some freshwater snails come to the surface of the water to breathe oxygen. Other freshwater snails have gills and take oxygen from the water.

## SEAWATER SNAILS

Seawater snails are the largest group of snails. They can be found along the coast or on the ocean floor. Most seawater snails have gills, and coloured and patterned shells.

A cowrie is a kind of sea snail. Cowries live in the Indian and Pacific Oceans.

**INTERESTING FACT**

Cone shells live in the sea. They have a poisonous sting to kill small fish for food. Cone shells can be harmful to humans.

## SLUGS ▼

A slug is a kind of snail without a shell. Brightly coloured sea slugs are often found in the shallow waters around coral reefs.

# SNAKE

SEE ALSO • Alligator • Animal • Lizard • Reptiles

A snake is a reptile. It is a long, legless animal that moves about by crawling. Snakes have dry, smooth skin. They are closely related to lizards.

## PARTS OF A SNAKE

A snake does not have ears. It can feel vibrations from the ground.

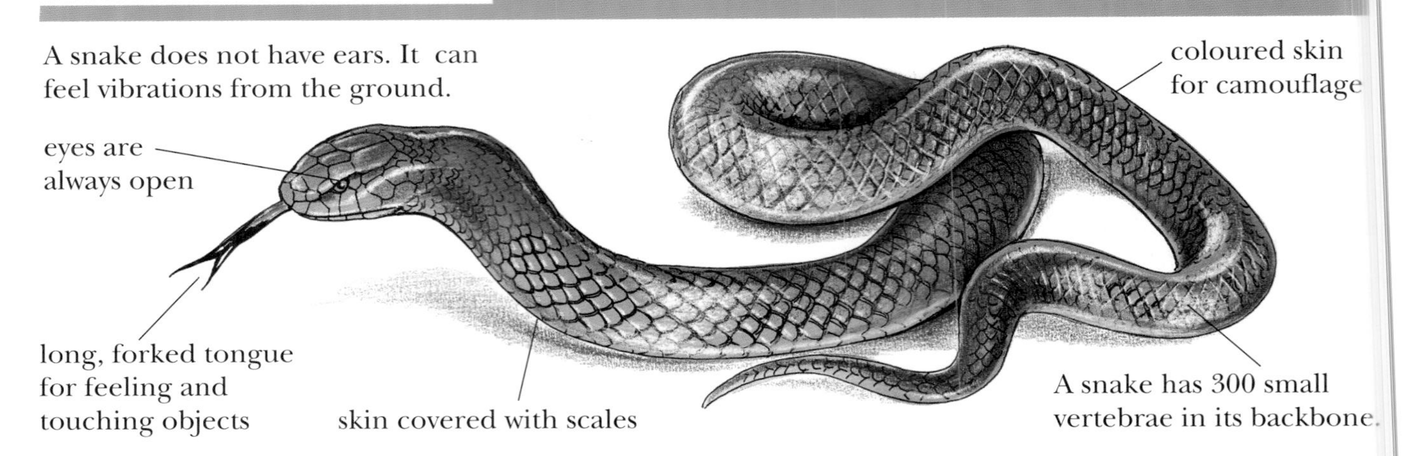


## FOOD

Snakes eat other animals. They are carnivores.

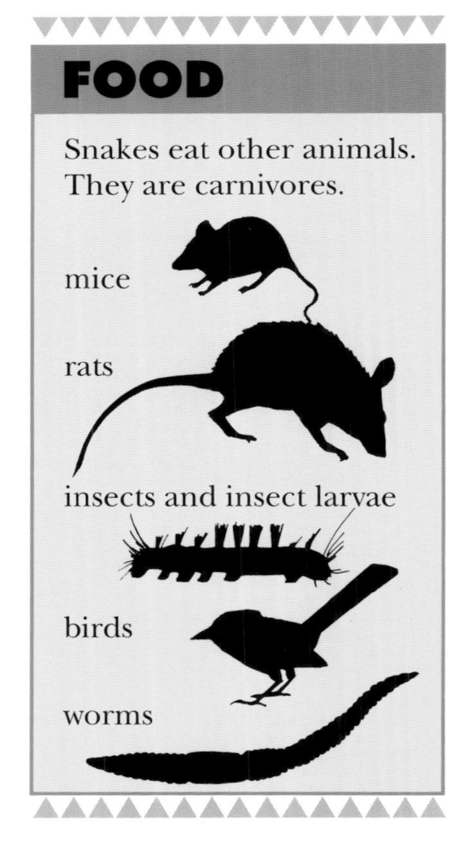

A snake swallows its food whole because it cannot chew. It can separate its jaws to swallow a whole animal. The snake digests all the animal except the feathers and hair.

## WHERE SNAKES LIVE

Snakes live in most parts of the world except the polar regions, New Zealand and other islands. Most snakes live in warm places. In colder places, snakes hibernate during the winter.

## HOW SNAKES LIVE

- Most snakes hatch from eggs.
- Some snakes, such as the garter snake, are born alive. Young snakes can take care of themselves.

## HOW SNAKES MOVE

Snakes wriggle their bodies along the ground and move their heads from side to side. Snakes can also climb and swim.

## POISONOUS SNAKES

Some snakes paralyse their prey with venom. The taipan uses its fangs to inject poison into its prey.

**INTERESTING FACT**

Snakes grow a new skin several times a year. They slip out of their old skin, leaving it inside out behind them.

## CONSTRICTORS ▶

Boas and pythons belong to a group of snakes called constrictors. They wrap themselves around their prey and suffocate it. Pythons are among the largest snakes. They can grow up to ten metres long.

# SOCCER

SEE ALSO • Football • Rugby

Soccer is a sport. In many parts of the world, soccer is called football. It is played with 2 teams of 11 players and a round ball. Players must not touch the ball with their hands or arms. Only the goalkeeper can touch the ball with his hands within the goal area.

## THE SOCCER FIELD

Soccer is played on a rectangular field. At each end of the field is the goal. Sometimes it has a net to catch the ball.

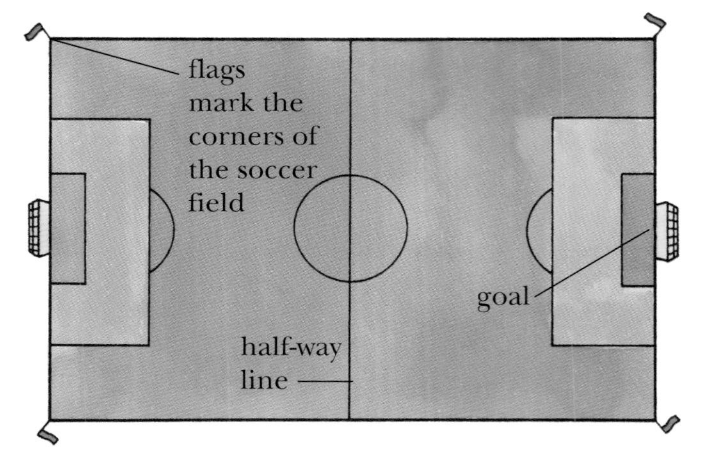


## EQUIPMENT

round leather ball

team uniforms – socks, shinguards, shorts, shirt

## TIME OF THE GAME

The game lasts 90 minutes with an interval at half time.

## ◄ SCORING

A team scores a goal when the ball passes into the other team's goal.

The World Cup is a major soccer competition. It is held every four years with teams competing from all over the world.

# SOUND

SEE ALSO • Bat • Ears • Music

Sound is made by the vibrations of an object. It travels in invisible waves. Sound comes from living and non-living things.

## HOW SOUND TRAVELS

Vibration of the air makes soundwaves travel in all directions. When you clap, air moves or vibrates. The vibrations make waves of sound travel outwards. Some of the soundwaves reach your ears. This makes your eardrums vibrate and hear the sound.

## VOCAL CHORDS

When you speak, air from your lungs causes your vocal chords to vibrate. This produces sound. Sound is carried on the air from your mouth. Frogs, birds and most mammals use vocal chords to make sounds.

## KINDS OF SOUNDS

Sounds can be loud or soft, high or low.

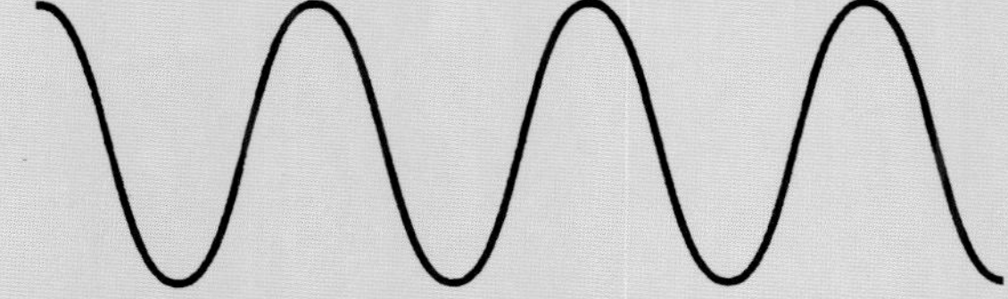

- High sounds are made by things that vibrate quickly.

- Low sounds are made by things that vibrate slowly.

# SPACECRAFT

SEE ALSO • Astronaut • Moon • Planet • Satellite • Space Shuttle

Spacecraft travel into space. Space probes, satellites, shuttles and rockets are spacecraft. They are launched into space by powerful rockets.

## MANNED SPACECRAFT

The American spacecraft Apollo II landed on the Moon in 1969. The command module for the astronauts was in the nose of the spacecraft. Apollo II carried scientific equipment as well as special equipment to keep the astronauts alive and well.

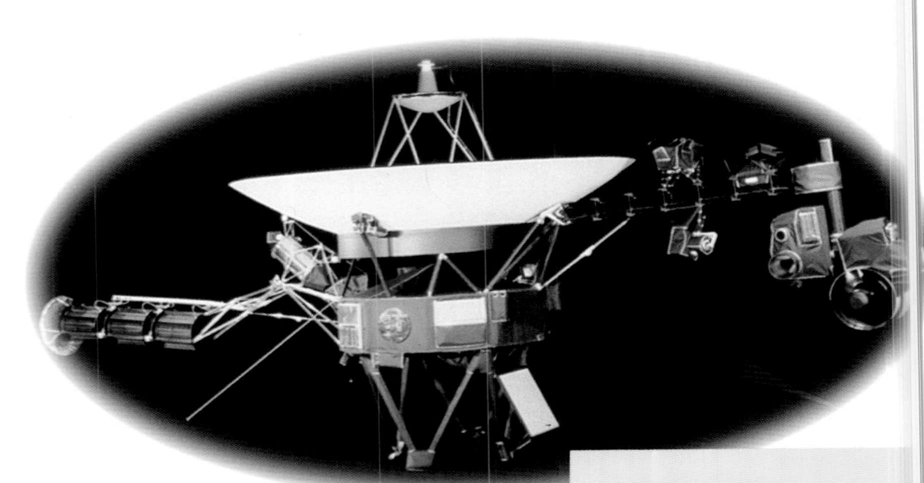

## SPACE ▲ PROBES

A space probe is an unmanned spacecraft. Space probes are used to collect photographs and information about the Earth, the other planets and space. The information and photographs are beamed back to the Earth by radio.

# SPACE SHUTTLE

SEE ALSO • Astronaut • Moon • Planet • Satellite • Spacecraft

A space shuttle is a spacecraft that can be used to travel into space many times.

rudder
scientific instruments are used to study outer space
rocket engines
flight deck
living quarters

4. The shuttle can launch satellites and space probes in space. They can pick up damaged satellites.

satellite

3. The fuel tank breaks away when it is empty.

fuel tank

5. The space shuttle slows down its orbit to return to Earth.

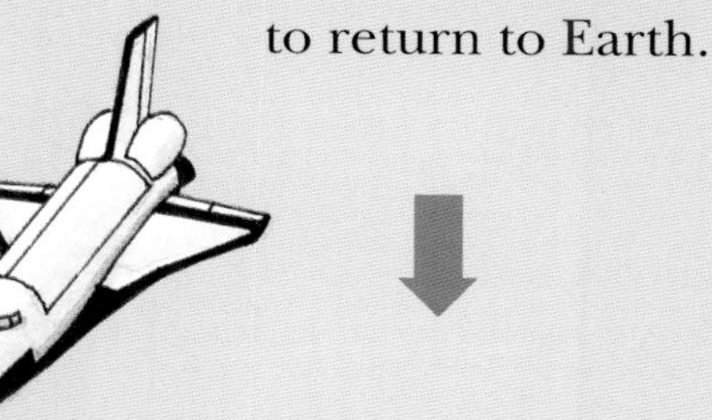

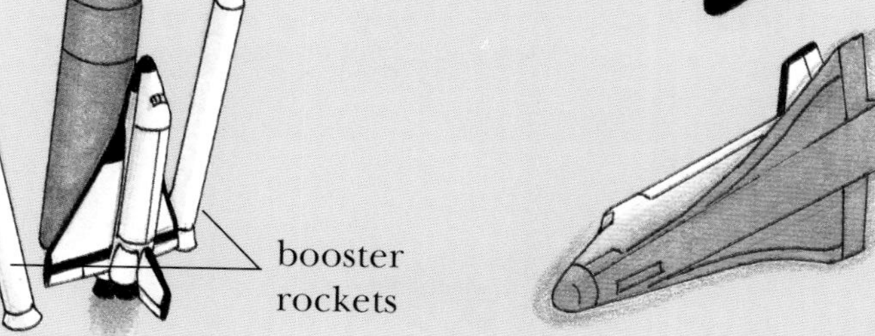


2. The booster rockets break away (fall off) as the shuttle climbs. They can be used again.

6. The space shuttle enters the Earth's atmosphere and air friction makes it glow red hot.

1. A space shuttle is launched by rocket.

7. The space shuttle lands like an aeroplane on a runway.

# SPIDER

SEE ALSO • Animal • Invertebrat

A spider is a small animal with eight legs. There are many different kinds of spiders. Each kind of spider is different in shape, colour and size.

## PARTS OF A SPIDER

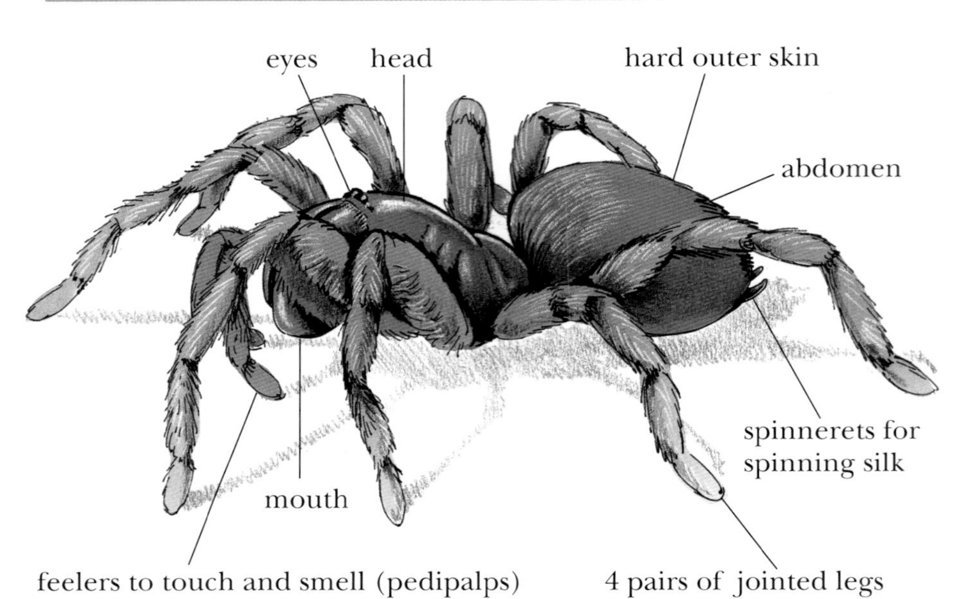


Spiders can have up to 8 eyes. The size, number and position of eyes change in different kinds of spiders.

## FOOD

Spiders eat other animals. They are carnivores.

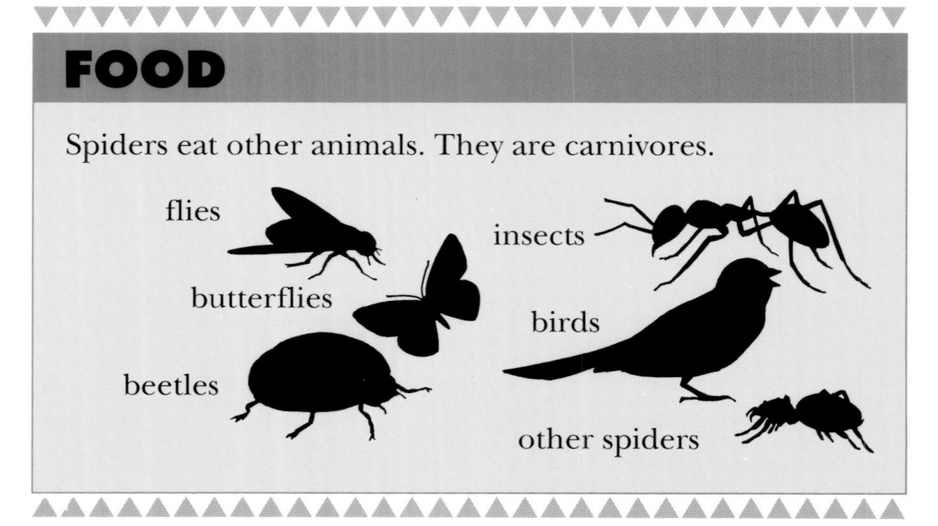


## SIZE OF SPIDERS

Spiders vary in size. The smallest spiders are about one millimetre wide. The South American bird-eating spider has a leg span of 30 centimetres.

## ARACHNIDS

Spiders, scorpions, ticks and mites belong to a group of animals called arachnids.

## WHERE SPIDERS LIVE

Spiders live all over the world, from the tops of trees to the soil on the ground.

## ORB WEAVERS ▶

Orb weavers are spiders that spin delicate webs. The sticky silk thread is laid in circles. The web is used to catch food. Some spiders wait nearby. Others wait in the centre of the web. Most orb web spiders spin a new web almost every day.

## HUNTING SPIDERS

Hunting spiders hunt for food. The trapdoor spider lays silk tripwires. It hides in a burrow and springs out if an insect triggers a tripwire.

## HOW SPIDERS LIVE

- Most female spiders spin an egg case in which they lay their eggs. The case protects the eggs. Some spiders carry the case until the eggs hatch. Some spiders suspend the egg case from silk threads. Some spiders wrap their egg case in a leaf and leave it on the ground.
- Spiderlings hatch from the eggs.

## POISONOUS SPIDERS

All spiders have fangs. Most spiders have poison glands. Spiders use their poison to kill insects. Some spiders such as the black widow produce poison which is harmful to humans.

# STAR

SEE ALSO • Astronomy • Galaxy • Sun • Telescope • Universe

A star is a burning ball of gas that shines in the night sky. Stars are made of two gases – hydrogen and helium. They produce huge amounts of heat and light.

◀ There are billions and billions of stars in our galaxy, the Milky Way.

## STARLIGHT

Stars look as though they are twinkling. As their light passes through the Earth's atmosphere, the light rays are bent. This makes them twinkle.

## CONSTELLATIONS

Long ago, people gave names to patterns of stars. The constellation of Orion was named after the hunter Orion in Greek mythology.

### INTERESTING FACT

Stars are a long way from the Earth. The star nearest to the Earth is the Sun. It takes eight minutes for the Sun's light to reach Earth. The next closest star is much further away. It takes four years for its light to reach Earth.

# SUBMARINE

SEE ALSO • Boat • Floating • Ship

A submarine is a boat that can travel under water. Some submarines carry torpedoes to attack ships. Others are used to explore under water.

STAR SUBMARINE

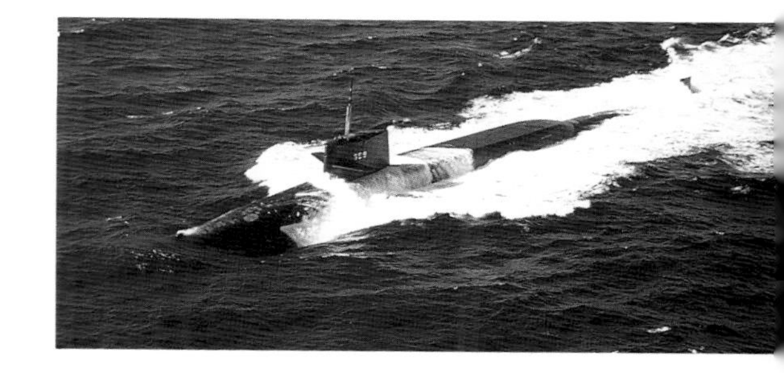

## PARTS OF A SUBMARINE

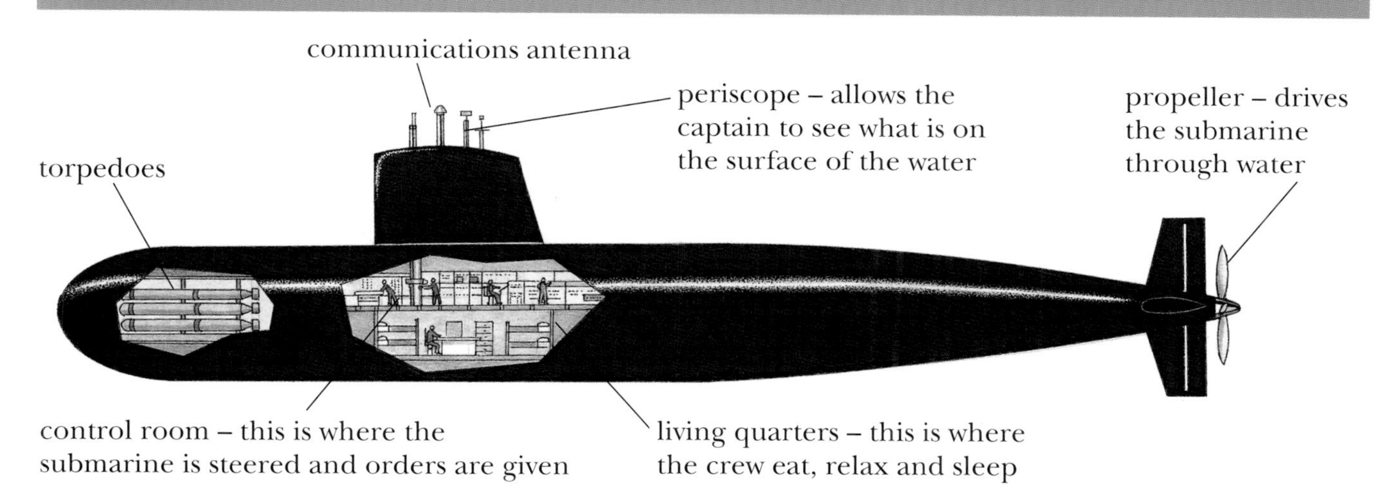


## HOW A SUBMARINE WORKS

A submarine has tanks called ballast tanks. The tanks can be filled with water or air, and emptied.

ballast tank

**To float**
The tanks are filled with air.

**To go down**
Water is pumped into the tanks and air is pumped out.

**To come back up**
Air is pumped into the tanks and water is forced out.

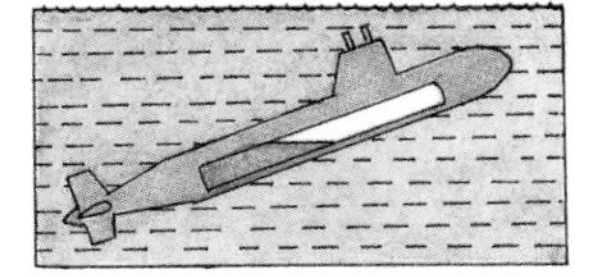

## HISTORY

The first submarine was made of wood. It was built by an American in 1775. It could only carry one person.

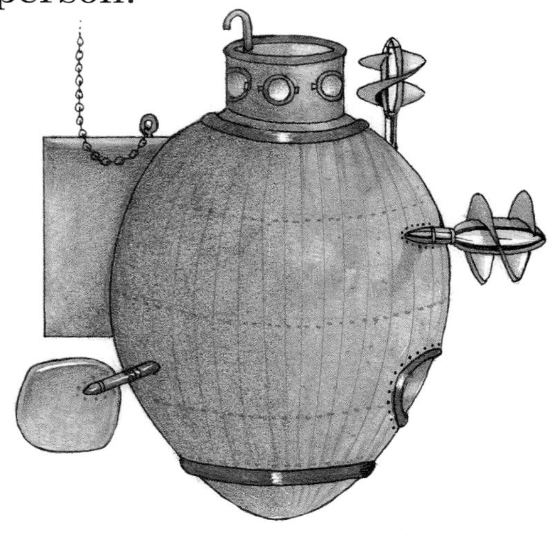

# SUN

SEE ALSO • Astronomy • Earth • Planet • Star • Weather

The Sun is a star. It is a glowing ball of gases. The Sun produces great amounts of light and heat.

The Sun is a huge ball of gas: 3/4 hydrogen and 1/4 helium.

Light from the Sun takes eight minutes to reach the Earth.

## THE SOLAR SYSTEM

The Sun is the centre of the solar system. The planets and their moons orbit the Sun. The Earth orbits the Sun once every year.

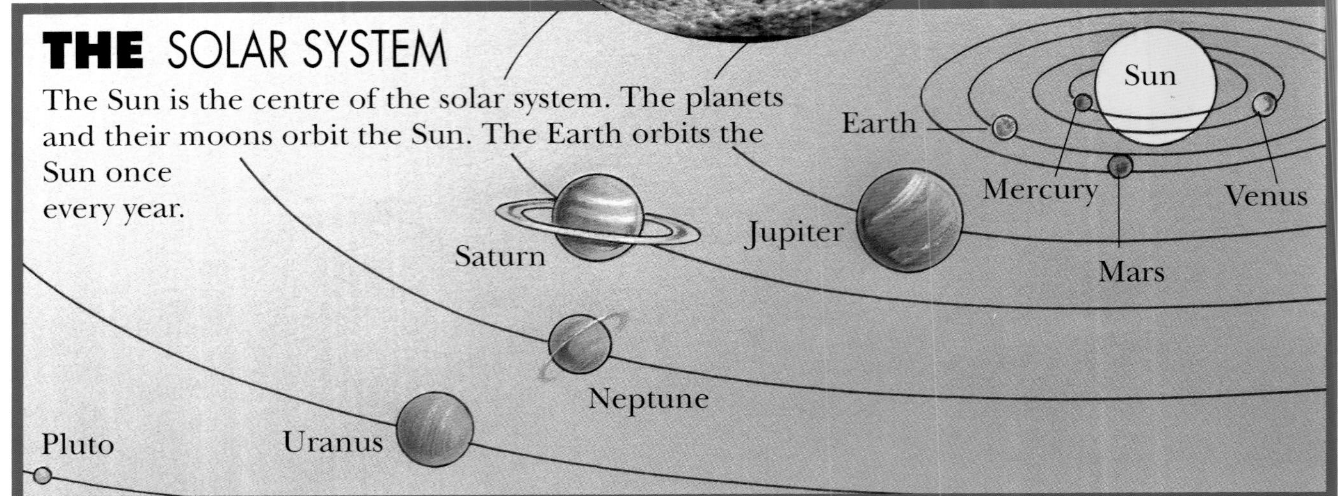

## THE SUN'S ENERGY

- Plants use the Sun's light to make food. Plants provide food for all life on Earth.
- The Sun warms the Earth. Without the Sun, the Earth would be frozen.
- The Sun heats the air and makes it move.
- The Sun makes water droplets evaporate into the air. When they cool, they fall as rain. Without the Sun, there would be no rain.

## SOLAR ENERGY

The Sun's energy can provide a safe, clean and cheap form of power. Solar cells made from silicon can change the Sun's light into electricity.